SUBHASH LAKHOTIA is one of India's top taxation experts and has practiced as a tax and investment consultant for more than forty years now. He is the Director of R. N. Lakhotia and Associates LLP and Lakhotia College of Taxation and Management.

Mr. Lakhotia has written numerous books on income tax, investment, real estate and spirituality. He is also the featured expert of the very popular television talk show, "Tax Guru" on CNBC Awaaz TV channel. The show has completed more than 300 episodes and won the National Television Award 2010 for the "Best Business Talk Show of the Year". Mr. Lakhotia has addressed hundreds of seminars and lecture meetings on taxation and tax planning. He also writes for many of India's leading newspapers and conducts the popular course known as "Zero to Hero in Direct Taxes".

In 1970, Subhash Lakhotia was selected as the best Indian youth by the Lions International to represent India at the World Youth Congress held at Atlantic City, USA. He is Secretary General of Investors Club and President of Spiritual Club International and Unite to Invest (UTI). He is Chief Strategist of the Real Estate Strategy Group and is actively associated with various professional bodies connected with real estate. He is actively associated with Lions Clubs International. He has been awarded the "Sahityashree" award and "The Suryadatta National Award, 2010". He is a member of the Governing Council of Proton Business School.

Dedicated

with utmost respect and regard
to my most venerable mother
late Shrimati Asha Rani Lakhotia.
It's due to her inspiration and encouragement
that I could write this book.

HOW TO BECOME A MULTI-MILLIONAIRE

Subhash Lakhotia
'Tax Guru' of CNBC-Awaaz,
Top Taxation and Investment Expert

www.visionbooksindia.com

Disclaimer

All investments are subject to risk. The author and the publisher disclaim all legal or other responsibilities for any losses which readers may suffer by investing or trading using the ideas or methods suggested in this book. Readers are advised to seek professional guidance before making any specific investments.

ISBN 10: 81-7094-830-4
ISBN 13: 978-81-7094-830-8

Published by
Vision Books Pvt. Ltd
(Incorporating Orient Paperbacks & CARING imprints)
24 Feroze Gandhi Road, Lajpat Nagar 3
New Delhi 110024, India.
Phone: (+91-11) 2983 6470 or 2983 6480
E-mail: visionbk@vsnl.com

Printed at
Anand Sons
C-88 Ganesh Nagar, Pandav Nagar Complex,
Delhi-110092, India.

Contents

Preface

It was my long cherished dream to write a book which would inspire India's younger generation to aim big and grow rich. Finally, after years of thinking and planning, here it is. This first of its kind book is intended for those young Indians who dreaming of becoming multi-millionaires and are ready to strive for achieving this goal.

If you, too, share the same dream, this book will instil in you the confidence to believe in yourself and to achieve something really big in your life. I assure you with my complete conviction that anyone can achieve big goals. If you have indomitable will-power and a strong passion for excellence, nobody in the world can stop you from becoming a multi-millionaire.

I have a strong belief that if the younger generation of today's entrepreneurs sincerely follows the guidelines and suggestions contained in this book, hundreds and thousands of them will become multi-millionaires very soon. And that, for me, would be the biggest reward of writing this book.

I thank my long-standing publisher, Kapil Malhotra, who has always encouraged me to write a book for larger social benefit. I would like to acknowledge that whatever I've learnt in life is due to my father, Shri Ram Niwas Lakhotia. It's his guidance and generosity that have made me what I'm today. I sincerely thank my wife Sushila Lakhotia, who has helped me in numerous ways to write this book and arrange the material in a proper way. Without her help, it would have been impossible for me to write it within a reasonable period of time.

My entire effort will be successful if younger Indian entrepreneurs find this book useful in their journey to becoming multi-millionaires. If you like this book, or if it somehow touches or inspires you, please do write and tell me so. Write to me about your journey to successful entrepreneurship and your valuable experiences in entering the multi-millionaire's club. These will serve as valuable examples to inspire countless others.

SUBHASH LAKHOTIA

1

Do You Really *Want to Be a Multi-Millionaire?*

The popular reality show on Indian television, "Kaun Banega Crorepati?" (Who Will Become a Multi-Millionaire?) became almost a national craze. It attracted participants from all walks of life, all aspiring to become multi-millionaires. People came from all over India to answer a long list of questions live on television. But only two among the hundreds of participants and thousands of aspirants, clinched the prize money of ten million rupees and actually became multi-millionaires.

This book is specially written for those who want to become multi-millionaires as quickly as possible. And, here, it does not involve a quiz with all its attendant uncertainty. Just strong will-power, tenacity, a few inner techniques and simple hard work are all it requires to reach the goal.

In fact, the motive for writing this book is to show how anyone can become a multi-millionaire, not just a select few. Success will be yours if you follow the guidelines and directions contained in this book; what you need to bring to the table are tenacity to pursue your dream and an abundance of bubbling enthusiasm.

Someone who aspires to become a multi-millionaire should never be discouraged by a dearth of resources; lack of money, education or opportunities. What you must have are a burning desire in your mind and big dreams in your eyes. As the legendary Walt Disney once said, "Don't dream small. If you are dreaming big, it will definitely materialize into reality."

Just dreaming big, though, is not enough; you should have the temperament and tenacity to make things happen. If you really want to be a multi-millionaire, take a pledge today that you won't ever stop midway and that you will never compromise with your dream. India alone boasts of scores of billionaires who made it happen by virtue of big dreams, bold plans and the will to prove their mettle in this world.

Think about it. What is it that they have and why are you lagging behind? A strong commitment, fierce conviction, unwavering persistence and an uncompromising attitude are what create multi-millionaires, nothing else. Only a few are born multi-millionaires, those born in leading business families, for example. But not being born rich doesn't stop a person from dreaming big and achieving great success.

Take the case of India's former President, A. P. J. Abdul Kalam. From a humble beginning, he rose to the pinnacle of power. Not just that. He is known as the father of India's missile technology. He is a constant inspiration for millions of people who want to make it big in their own lives. He always says: Aim for the stars!

Think higher, reach higher, that's the secret of progress in life. Don't get entrapped in the dreams and the humdrum reality of an ordinary life.

Remember that saying: God helps those who help themselves. So, if you want to become a multi-millionaire, it's time to think big and engage in big activities. Envision yourself as a multi-millionaire a few years from now — and prepare yourself accordingly. The joy of big accomplishments will then soon crown your life.

Of course, there will be obstacles and adversaries aplenty along the way. Sometimes you will find yourself in seemingly hopeless situations and think of quitting the pursuit of prosperity mid-way. But a quitter never wins and a winner never quits, is the basic motto of growth and of all big achievements. Never let yourself feel dejected and defeated. You are not defeated, until you accept defeat. Your pursuit should be genuine and sincere. There should be no second thought or change of course mid-way. Temporary setbacks and defeats are quite normal, don't take them to be the end result.

If sometimes you find yourself mentally and emotionally let down and dejected, read inspirational books. They will lift up your mood and spirits. I would suggest that you should read the complete writings of Swami Vivekananda, available in ten volumes. They are a real treasure trove of inspiration which everyone can afford. There is something in the writings of the magnificent Swami which can ignite the hidden power which lies within everyone, dispel the clouds of gloominess in your mind and make one tough as tempered steel, keenly prepared for bigger achievements in life.

This is not just my belief; it's the truth. Over the years, I've received hundreds of letters and messages from people who have made it big in their lives, money-wise or otherwise. They have written to me that in their hours of despair, the writings of Swami Vivekananda kept the fire burning in their souls, lifted their thoughts to inspiring heights, and, almost like a miracle, helped bring them back to the centre of activities and achievement. Your mind becomes empowered, your thoughts become unified and effective, and your actions get directed by indomitable will-power towards higher goals. Such is the power of Swami Vivekananda's writings and thoughts.

Another inspirational treasure that can help you achieve your goals in the most powerful and certain way is *The Bhagavad Gita*. Over the ages, the *Bhagavad Gita* has inspired millions of people — leaders, entrepreneurs, management maestros, the big dreamers and common people alike. Each and every chapter of the *Gita* can guide a person in his or her pursuit of bigger goals. I suggest that every aspiring multi-millionaire should use it as a guidebook in his or her pursuit of prosperity.

Vedas have been the enduring source of inspiration for Indians and others alike. The Germans were the first Westerners to seek the knowledge of the Vedas to fortify their lives with the inspirational ideas of these great books. English and Swedish translations further spread their message of exhilaration and fortitude to the West. Today, thousands of foreigners are reaching for this source of immortal knowledge for guidance in their lives.

Let a Vedic mantra lead you in your pursuit of power, prosperity and happiness everyday. If you are an aspiring multi-millionaire, make it a point to dedicate a few minutes to meditation and the chanting of an inspirational Vedic mantra and see the difference it makes. It will help focus your mind, free it of useless clutter, and empower it for higher achievements.

ओ म शन्नो देवीरभिष्टय आपो भवन्तु पीतय।
शंयोरभिस्रवन्तु नः।
यजु. 36.12

Let the divine water be healing, helping and fit for drinking to us.
Let healing and blessing flow towards us.
Yaju 36.12

In the last forty years of my professional life, I've seen the power of the *Gayatri Mantra* in bringing success and prosperity into the lives of many successful businessmen. Chanting the *Gayatri*, or any other mantra of your choice, prior to any important appointment, meeting or transaction works wonders without fail. All you need are a few undisturbed minutes to concentrate your mind, a quiet corner in your office or at your home and an open, unprejudiced mind. It does not cost you any money but it will work wonders for you in helping you achieve your dreams. It prepares you to accept the abundance of nature, which includes material prosperity.

If you aspire to be a multi-millionaire, never boast of your dream with arrogance. Instead, steadfastly prepare your mind for your goal. Your strong will-power, tenacity and burning desire will show you both the way and the means. If you are determined and unwavering in your purpose, no power on earth can stop you from reaching your goal.

Once I was passing through Bank Street in the Karol Bagh area of New Delhi. This road is known for its endless rows of jewellery shops. It's the hub for the sale and purchase of precious metals and stones in the whole of India. Hordes of women come here to shop for the latest designs of jewellery.

Not surprisingly, I was stuck in a traffic jam in the crowded road, idly drumming my fingers on the steering wheel. Nothing moved for quite some time, so I had those idle moments to watch and observe the goings-on in detail. I saw an electric wire precariously strung overhead between two lamp posts on the opposite sides of the crowded street. A horde of monkeys was merrily crossing the street high up above the jam packed road, traipsing across that flimsy electric wire. Inspired by the monkeys, a lone squirrel then scurried across the wire and crossed over, probably hunting for food. I was immediately struck by how there are always ways around a seeming impasse, if only one has the tenacity to try whatever it takes. Nothing can then stop a person from achieving his or her dreams.

There is another incident I still vividly remember. I was sitting in our garden after dinner and chatting with other family members. A lone kitten attracted my attention It was trying to jump on to the top of our boundary wall in order to get to the road outside It was a small kitten and our boundary wall is at least five feet high. After three, four, five futile attempts, I thought I should open the main gate to let it out. But the kitten suddenly surprised everyone. It made a fresh attempt, this time from quite some distance, and was successfully able to jump on to the top of the wall! It struck me then that if someone has such tenacity and willingness to keep trying, nothing can stop that person from reaching his or her goals.

Saving is a basic prerequisite for becoming a multi-millionaire. If you don't save, you are jeopardising your future prosperity. Whether it be your business or your family make it a point never to buy unnecessary things. It's better to save, instead. Recently, I met a highly successful family of entrepreneurs who made it big even in economically troublesome times. They told me that they had focused on saving and succeeded in putting a halt on unnecessary expenditure. They negotiated very hard for every purchase and ultimately saved a lot of money, which came quite handy for their business growth. If you are aspiring to be a multi-millionaire, learn the art of saving and spending prudently.

No, I'm not advocating miserliness or penny-pinching. What I'm suggesting is that you must evaluate the justification of every item of expenditure. If you can do that diligently, it will help you both to pre-empt and solve various financial problems that inevitably recur from time to time. If you can control your expenditure successfully, it will make you an accomplished businessman.

Another valuable point is to always think positively. Problems come and go; they are transient and pass away. They are the testing measures for growth. Never get overly perturbed by difficulties in your life; focus, instead, on solutions. You must learn to keep away all negative thoughts from your mind.

In 1970, Lions International organized a contest to select a youth to represent India in the World Youth Congress which was to be held in USA. When I saw the advertisement, I too thought of taking part in the competition. To be frank, I was not very fluent in speaking English in those days. I had studied in Hindi-medium schools all along. Also my family background and upbringing was not such that I could be compared with the brightest and smartest young personalities from all over India. After all, it was a competition to select the best young personality to represent India on a global platform. My expectations were not too high but I thought it would be wonderful if I could get a free flight to America, free accommodation and food and a tour around the country.

As it happened, from among thousands of participants from India, Nepal and Burma, I was selected as the Ambassador of Goodwill to represent India as well as entire South Asia. That very day it was permanently etched on my mind that we can achieve whatever that we wish for very strongly and sincerely.

This is why I have this strong belief that anyone can become a multi-millionaire. The condition is, one should wish for it with true conviction, and keep on moving towards the goal with utmost persistence. And, of course, the ways and means you adopt must be honest and above board, otherwise it's of no use. Millions earned by unfair means can't give you prestige, peace of mind or stability. We want people who are hard working, enthusiastic and committed. People of whom relatives, friends and associates can be proud.

I would like to mention here another episode from my life. A few years ago I was watching a popular programme on the CNBC-Awaaz TV Channel. It was a programme based on people's day-to-day problems of personal finance. The half-hour programme was hosted by one of America's most popular female TV anchors. But the programme did not convince me. The entire programme revolved around credit card debt and divorce-related problems. Of course, these two are very common in USA. But, in India's context, it was somehow out of tune and exaggerated. Even today, divorce and credit card problems are not commonplace in India. I called up a friend and told him so. He, too, agreed.

Suddenly a thought came to my mind and I immediately wrote a letter to the TV channel. I said that the programme's focus was not relevant to the Indian context, and putting it on the TV channel for half an hour, discussing solely US problems, did not suit Indian needs. I suggested to them that instead they should telecast personal finance and tax related programmes based on practical Indian situations. I also humbly suggested that, if asked to, I was ready to conduct such a programme for them.

At that time I had no experience of conducting a television programme. Also, I had no godfather in the media. I don't know what happened at the management level at CNBC-Awaaz but the channel agreed to my proposal and asked me to anchor the programme for them. That was the beginning of my enormously popular TV programme, "Tax Guru". For several years in a row now it's remained one of the most popular programmes on CNBC-Awaaz.

What I m trying to say is quite simple — never hesitate to take a new step. Never get bogged down in thinking about possible negative outcomes to a new initiative. If you have a burning desire to do something, you are bound to be successful.

What is your life's purpose? What is your goal? Ask yourself seriously these two fundamental questions.

I've written something about the importance of asking oneself these two questions which I often repeat in my lectures:

> What is the purpose of your life? Where do you want to go? Without a purpose, your life is aimless, rudderless. You will never know the real joy of life until you are successful in fulfilling your dreams, reaching your goal! Merry-making just gives momentary happiness, but if you want a continuously happier state of mind for your whole life, wake up to your life's true purpose and fulfil it.

Don't be disheartened if you are not yet a multi-millionaire. Get inspiration from those who have made it big in their lives. Read their biographies or autobiographies — and get inspired and guided by them.

The life of J. K. Rowling, Harry Potter's creator, is a real life rags-to-riches fairy tale. Before becoming world famous, Rowling was struggling with poverty and a broken marriage. She used to write sitting for hours in inexpensive pubs because she had no heating system at home and her two-year old daughter was able to sleep cosily the pub's sofa. She received lots of rejections for her manuscript, but she never lost heart. Ultimately, her persistence worked and today she is one of the richest people in the world.

The founder of IKEA, the world renowned Swedish ready-to-assemble furniture business, is another such person. Born in an ordinary family, no one expected much of him. But a small investment from nominal prize money offered by his father, plus sheer hard work and years of persistence made him one of the richest people in the world.

And there is this other person whose mother died when he was just nine years old. There was no one at home to care for him. He used to cook for his office-going father and himself. After his father left for office, he had to clean the house, the kitchen and the dishes and at the same time study by himself. The nondescript one-room accommodation they had rented cost just two rupees a month. There was no electric light, no running water, nor a table where he could study. He used to study under the street lights or in the park outside, and often sit in the poorly-lit staircases to study. No one helped him in his studies. Yet he stood first in his class, passed all the exams, including M.Com and LLB in First Class, and his name featured in the merit list.

He is my father, R.N. Lakhotia, who has the rare honour of having written the maximum number of income tax related books in the world. When I ask him about the inspiration behind his exemplary success, he always tells me that it's his strong will-power and determination that helped him all along. He strongly believes that whatever power and support one needs to be successful are already within oneself. One has only to summon them to fulfil one's dreams.

Once when I was in Ahmedabad to address a seminar, I met one of the biggest hoteliers of Gujarat. This gentleman started his life as an ordinary helper in his father's roadside tea stall. Today he is one of the most respected entrepreneurs and a member of several important entrepreneur bodies.

So, my friends, very few people are born multi-millionaires. Most have made it on their own through their sheer persistence, hard work and a never-say-die attitude. First, make up your mind. Take a pledge today that you want to be a multi-millionaire. Nothing in this world can then stop you from reaching your goal.

Who says that everyone is not destined to be a multi-millionaire? People who think like that are pessimists. If you have the will, the determination, ability to work hard and a defined goal, the fate lines will automatically start acting to favour you. Unless and until you try, how can you know which door will open for you at what time. Thoughts are powerful and so is the tenacity of will-power. The only thing to remember is that there is no short cut to success. And, above all, your wishes should be genuine and your means above board. Never let greed overcome your honest intentions.

After many years of tremendous success and fame, the Indian matinee idol Amitabh Bachchan had to pass through a bad patch. His films flopped at the box office one after the other, his newly started production company fell flat on its face, his political career was smeared with scandals, his financial luck seemed to run out and, ultimately, his mortgaged house was on the verge of being auctioned off to pay for his debts.

But he never lost his fighting spirit. He embarked on relatively small-time advertising assignments, unimportant roles in films and ultimately into television anchoring. One such assignment was anchoring the earlier-mentioned TV programme, "Kaun Banega Crorepati?" which became a landmark in the history of Indian television.

In this book, I've tried to convey to you a very simple fact: Yes, You Can Be a Multi-Millionaire!

And not just a few of you. But each and every one of you! And that's my dream.

I hope this book will realize the dreams of many Indians, or every Indian, thus realizing my dream, too!

2

Saving Makes a Multi-Millionaire

Whether you are running a business or starting one, saving should always be a priority. An ingrained habit of saving is the first sign of a prospective multi-millionaire. In every facet of running a business, saving should be at the top of your agenda.

Of course, you must spend on new technology and acquisitions but there should be no unnecessary or useless spending. Every penny spent should be well spent for the success of your business alone.

In this one can emulate the thrifty buying habits of a housewife. When shopping for fruit or vegetables, a housewife first visits different shops to compare prices, bargains hard and only when satisfied that she has obtained the best deal does she make her purchases. When shopping at the shopping malls or at departmental stores, a housewife considers many factors, such as who is offering the highest discount, which shop has an ongoing "sale", who is offering free gifts, etc. Purchasing an item only after ensuring that she has struck the best bargain ensures that ultimately she saves the most. Such a method should be considered a best practice for business as well. The mantra "save at every point" applies rigorously to an aspiring multi-millionaire.

While buying office supplies, raw material or machinery for the business, or when redecorating office space, you must thoroughly investigate the suppliers, their pricing, comparative market rates, available discounts and bargains before finalizing the deals. This saving of your hard earned money will greatly help you realize your dreams of becoming a multi-millionaire.

Every penny saved becomes a valuable resource for the success of a business. Every successful businessman knows this basic rule of success.

Let me consider a simple example. Suppose you are a budding businessman going for a business trip. Making saving your prime concern, you must search for the most economical airlines, the cheapest fare, or a travel agent who can give you maximum discount, or find airlines which give ultra cheap prices if tickets are booked well in advance.

The same logic applies to hotel booking as well. When your business is small, any economy class hotel should be fine for you. Never go in for a luxury hotel at an exorbitant cost just to impress others or to show off.

These are just examples but I hope my message is clear. If you make it a habit to save more, your journey to becoming a multi-millionaire will happen that much quicker.

It's like your childhood piggybank. Each and every paisa you save, builds up to become a substantial enough amount to buy a toy or a children's book. A determined saver today is the multi-millionaire of tomorrow!

In India, we are big social spenders. Marriages are multi-million affairs. Not for nothing is the especially lavish Indian marriage dubbed "the big fat Indian wedding". Birthdays, anniversaries, inauguration of showrooms or offices, every occasion is seen as a big opportunity to show off. If you want to be a multi-millionaire then you must get rid of this mind set.

Let me give a practical example. If you are not a big businessman, why do you need a bigger car? Just to show off? It doesn't lead you anywhere. It is just unnecessary cost.

If an important foreign collaborator or buyer visits you and you need a big car to impress him, you can always hire a super luxury car for a day or two. The cost of maintaining a big car is much, much higher than hiring the top-most latest luxury car for a day or two.

When you learn to save, you earn! You need that earning to run your business smoothly, to ward off any future trouble in your business. There is a wise saying which encapsulates this approach, "A stitch in time saves nine".

And the rule should be the same for everyone in your company; your business partner, your manager, your workers — everyone!

Spending on acquiring new technology and know-how is quite justified. No one will question your wisdom in doing so. But you should learn to differentiate between justified expenses and unnecessary ones. This discrimination marks out a highly successful businessman from the unsuccessful one.

Here I would like to give an example from my personal life.

In 1964, my father resigned from the post of an Income Tax officer and joined the Birla Group. He used to get two thousand rupees as his salary, one thousand rupees each from two different Birla Group companies.

From the very first month, he would put away one salary in a bank account and used only the other to run his family. Yes, life was not that comfortable, hardships were there but he never forgot to save half of his total earnings. Today the family reaps the huge benefit of his prudent decision.

Alas, the trend is different today. We often hear about young people earning lakhs of rupees every month but they spend almost all of their salary in buying luxury goods, gadgets, branded clothes, expensive cars, etc. As a result, their savings are almost nil.

But if you are an aspiring multi-millionaire, your success mantra should be, save, save and save! Whatever be the situation, constraint or compulsion, never forget to save. Who knows what lies in the future? Savings are your safety valves for times of crisis and emergency. Savings protect you from going bankrupt, from dependence on others and from uncertainty. These savings will ultimately save you, the future of your business, and your dreams. A multi-millionaire is also a multi saver. This is the proven path to success — and there is no short cut to it.

3

The Magical Padta *System of the Marwaris*

By the middle of the 20th century, some Marwari families in Kolkata were already multi-millionaires. They had come to the city with very few resources, often having just about enough to barely survive. By and large, they were poorly educated and without any special qualifications. The qualities they did possess were a willingness to work hard and the zeal to become multi-millionaires.

In hindsight, it seems almost impossible. No degree, no special qualification, no job experience — nothing! Who would offer them jobs, what would be their means for survival . . . everything was uncertain. But they not only survived, they flourished, becoming millionaires and multi-millionaires in the course of time.

These families, who arrived in hordes to an alien city from their native homes in Rajasthan in the post-Partition era, had decided that "We shall overcome". Their dogged determination helped them to survive in the toughest of situations. They faced it all, misfortune, drawbacks, severe financial crunch, lack of education, threadbare resources and yet they ultimately triumphed. Most of these families are now multi-millionaires.

When I studied their success strategy closely, I found that it was neither miracle nor super human endeavour — rather, there was a time-tested formula behind their success. It's unique and unparalleled. And it's known as the *Padta* system in common parlance.

Now, what is this *Padta* system?

It's a system that started long before there were computers or calculators. A Marwari businessman would make a detailed calculation of the probable cost, profit and loss of a new business venture on a plain piece of paper and compare it with the prevailing market rates of return. Only if the prospective returns satisfied him, would he proceed with that business venture. This common sense practice is termed as the *Padta* system.

In cities like Kolkata and Mumbai, highly ambitious Marwari entrepreneurs depended on this basic formula of success. And it was a hit. The time-tested formula brought them success, making them multi-millionaires within a few years.

In a nutshell, the *Padta* system is a detailed pre-estimation of the likely profit and loss from a new business venture which acts as a guide map for the entrepreneur. You can call it a feasibility report or a cost-benefit analysis in the simplest form, but this simple calculation is the basis of many Indian business empires.

Even in today's changed business milieu and conditions, the *Padta* system works well; in fact, with almost 100 per cent effectiveness!

So, if you are entering a new venture or starting a new project or a factory, my suggestion is that you first make your own *Padta*. And cross check it carefully. The estimation you have made of sales, costs, profit margin and other ingredients of your business should be properly weighed.

Wishes are not everything. You need a road map and tenacity to follow it. The *Padta* system is such a valuable guide map for you. Follow it carefully, work hard and with strong determination to achieve your goal. You will never be a failure. The tested *Padta* system will help you achieve the best results and make you a multi-millionaire soon.

Why do many successful businessmen fail in their new venture? Why do some highly ambitious endeavours by star businessmen fail? There is a simple reason behind it. The *Padta* system was not employed.

An unexpected loss, when you were expecting a profit not only halts your momentum, it also kills your enthusiasm. So make sure that every time you enter a new business, a *Padta* is made and tested beforehand.

This system is religiously followed by scores of highly successful businessmen, India-wide. And, there must be a reason why they do so.

It hardly matters whether you run a small or a big enterprise. *Padta* fits into every business and budget quite well. If you are running a project employing hundreds of employees for months, and ultimately find yourself in a loss making situation, spending most of the resources on men and material, blame it on the absence of a *Padta* before you started the venture.

As an aspiring multi-millionaire you must do proper justice to your time, energy and resources by making a proper *Padta*, before starting any ambitious venture. Do it properly and cross-check it, and if it is convincing enough, there is no looking back.

Take this powerful mantra from the Marwari way of success to heart and success will surely follow.

4

Quit India!

You might find the title of this chapter a bit surprising and outlandish.

I was supposed to tell you the ways and means of becoming a multi-millionaire quickly, and here I am suggesting that you quit India to realize your dreams.

Actually, what I'm saying is that in this era of globalization, when the entire world is fast becoming a global village, you should try to go beyond your known pastures to make more money, using your talent and expertise.

Now the problem is you may have no knowledge of the laws and their intricacies in other countries. It is not easy to know what business will suit you well in a foreign land. Moreover, the world goes through periodic economic volatility. What would be a profitable business opportunity in such a scenario?

But this is exactly the opportunity.

For example, land and property prices in many Western European countries and in USA fell considerably after 2008. There were then plenty of properties available at much lower rates. So, if you can give the property business a try, becoming a multi-millionaire won't remain a distant dream.

Whenever such crises recur, go there, contact local banks in those countries and get a list of properties available for sale as a result of default and other reasons. Most probably, the banks will be eager to help you locate such properties as the number of defaulters is large at such times and banks are desperate to get rid of their liabilities. A ready channel for investors, who want to take the challenge, thus opens up in many countries.

If possible, join hands with your friends and partners. This will assure bigger investments and far better opportunities. Of course, you may not get immediate returns, but wait a little, maybe a year or two, let the market regain confidence. You will eventually find that what you have purchased are virtual goldmines! Cheaper but bigger properties along the seaside will be the best bet. If there is any such property available, buy it yourself or along with your business partners and start building a resort. Once you do this, there will be several multi-millionaires in the making within an incredibly short period of time.

Who knows, one successful business may lead to many others.

It's a known fact that most governments in developed countries encourage foreign investment in their countries, and legally there is not much difficulty in purchasing properties abroad. The Indian Foreign Exchange Management Act 1999 (FEMA) allows every individual Indian to invest two lakh US Dollars every year in properties abroad. And if you get together a group of friends and co-investors, the amount becomes larger. If planned and executed properly, no one can then stop you from becoming a multi-millionaire.

Of course, you should examine each and every case minutely before entering into a deal. You can hire lawyers, assessors and investigators to check every angle of a foreign property before buying it. Also, in most developed countries the related documents are available on the Net.

In many African and Latin American countries, agricultural land is available at much cheaper rates than it is in India. Buying such land through collective investment will be one of the most prudent decisions today and will reap big profits tomorrow. Farming on foreign soil is not a dream any more. You will be surprised to know that many Indian companies have already bought big chunks of agricultural land in foreign countries. And the available price of agricultural land is much, much cheaper than that in India.

For major business houses world-wide, this has become one of the most profitable investments these days. Many Chinese are also now making such investments.

So, if you are dreaming of becoming a multi-millionaire quickly, invest in farmland abroad. The same parameter applies to land around new or upcoming airports, developing tourist spots, etc. And do it when the prices are cheap and affordable.

Today, buying land in India, especially agricultural land, is a costly proposition. In the last few years there has been much development in the realty sector and so a lot of agricultural land has been developed into residential and commercial properties in Indian cities and smaller towns. Buying big chunks of farmland is next to impossible for individual investors now.

But huge tracts of agricultural land can still be bought in foreign countries. Also, it is cheaper. Just make up your mind, broaden your horizons, keep a constant watch on such available properties and contact the embassies and consulates in India for further information on procedures, local conditions, rules, regulations and modalities. Whether there is any local land ceiling rule applicable, whether there are rebates and tax holidays available or not — keep yourself updated with the facts and figures.

In India, usually 5 to 10 per cent stamp duty is levied on properties at the time of registration. This amount varies from state to state. Also there are ceilings on buying agro land. Which means a single owner can't buy unlimited stretch of lands, even if it comes cheaper.

Perhaps many of us do not know that buying agricultural land is an extremely lucrative proposition in the United States. There are states where stamp duty on agricultural land is almost negligible or there is no charge at all! Also, agricultural land in USA is exempted from house tax. It is exempted from property tax, too.

Isn't this a tempting scenario?

When investing in land overseas, find out if there are any further exemptions and relaxations. You will ultimately find that offshore properties are better options and bigger opportunities for prospective Indian multi-millionaires

Another important point is the Indian Income Tax Act has special provisions for exemptions and rebates on agricultural income. And there is no mention that income from agriculture has to be from within Indian territory alone.

Now, let us look at practicalities. How would you earn? I would suggest that if buy agricultural land in USA, do so in the outskirts of the towns and cities, at a distance of, say, 25-50 kilometres. In USA, even the smaller towns, semi-urban areas and rural areas are well connected by roads.

Farm for sometime on your acquired land and then gradually turn it into residential land. Of course, the conversion process should be carried out legally. Also be ready to pay house tax thereafter.

Divide the land into smaller plots. Build cottages or luxury residential hubs, with recreational facilities, such as clubs, pubs, sports courts, and the like. You will then see a substantial leap in property prices. Also, people living in the cities who are eager to buy a country house, will flock to you, making you a multi-millionaire.

You can consider collaborating with a US family in your project. This will add credibility to your venture.

You can also develop properties for NRIs in foreign countries, if you don't have contacts with foreigners. It would undoubtedly give the NRIs a feeling of Indian-ness in a foreign country. Comfortable surroundings, people from India living around, cultural, religious and recreational activities based on Indian themes, namely a Little India in foreign shores! If you can build such specialized properties, they will have higher demand among NRI communities. This will ultimately make you a successful entrepreneur abroad, and undoubtedly a multi-millionaire.

Where there is a will, there is a way. I should say, a thousand and one ways.

5

London to Ladnun: The Multi-millionaire's Trail

Who doesn't know about London. But, Ladnun? Where is that? No, there is no connection or comparison between the two places. They are different and distant, separated by thousands of kilometres. I'm citing Ladnun as merely an inspiration for earning millions. But, how?

I visited an exhibition at Pragati Maidan Exhibition Complex in New Delhi. A London-based company put up a big stall at the exhibition to attract Indian investors to London. They were seeking investors to invest in the realty sector near London. Plots were on sale and there was a heavy rush of prospective investors at the stall.

The crowds did not consist merely of curious onlookers. Many visitors came prepared and finalised the paperwork right there at the stall. And, within a matter of days the exhibitor had realised more than the targeted investment for the off-London properties which sold like hot cakes. Obviously, the company was very happy.

Clearly, in this era of globalization Indian businessmen too would like to make their presence felt overseas, particularly in a city such as London. Many owners of family-run business houses invested with the sole purpose of impressing people in their social circle with an address in London.

When I read the publicity brochure distributed by the company at their stall minutely, something unusual came to my notice. They were not offering prime property within the London metropolitan area. In fact, it was highlighted in bold letters that the land being offered was far off from the city, beyond existing residential areas. The area was not permitted to have any construction and no building plans would be sanctioned by the authorities at present.

But there was just one assurance. In future, "there is possibility" of regularization and permissions. Yes, the possibility was there, though it was a distant possibility.

How easily they had been able to sell big dreams to Indian investors! There was one lesson, a very important one, which I learnt from the episode. You can sell anything if you can excite people's imagination.

If a Londoner can sell nondescript land in a distant country to Indians, nothing stops us from doing the same to moneyed foreigners. Can't we sell agricultural land, say in Ladnun, or elsewhere, in the vicinity of major Indian cities and towns? The overseas investors can be assured that what today seem to be far-off areas would be the goldmines of tomorrow.

Taking part in property expos abroad and presenting semi-urban Indian land as a future money spinner, undoubtedly needs some courage but it also needs a far-sighted vision about one's business plan and financial goals.

When you are selling these properties, believe me, you are not doing anything wrong, neither are you telling lies. You must make it clear in your publicity literature that the land would not get immediate building permission but you can hold out the assurance of future possibilities.

What seems unexciting today can hold great promise in the future. So what if the off-London properties which people bought are not within any residential area or master plan. They are legal properties. The current constraint is that no building plan, no construction for the present but the investment is safe and secured. The plot remains in possession, waiting for future change in any city extension project. Who knew that Vashi in Mumbai, Dwarka in Delhi or Rajarhat in Kolkata would be such flourishing sub-cities as they have now become, with skyrocketing land prices.

Indian cities are bursting at their seams with ever-growing population. But the existing land area of the cities remains fixed. So, what do governments do? They extend the city area, plan sub-cities or new cities around existing cities. In this manner, over a period of time no area remains untouched by progress or development. Only, there is a gestation period. If one can wait out that time, there is no looking back.

So, selling land in Ladnun to Londoners can be a lucrative business proposal. Build your marketing team, an informative website, release advertisements, print high quality brochures and take part in property exhibitions, both in India and abroad. Make a team of 8-10 reliable business partners. Create a property bank of the plots available in the vicinity of various Indian cities. Earmark the locations. Go abroad. Put stalls in exhibitions and sell the land to NRIs and foreigners who have money and want to invest for lucrative future returns. Once you convince them, no one can stop your cash flow. Selling Indian hinterland to buyers assuring them of big future gains will make you a multi-millionaire almost overnight.

This is newly invented wealth making route. Keep looking for such innovative ideas to grow rich.

6

New Thinking in Agriculture Can Make You a Multi-Millionaire

The younger generation of rural Indians is not interested in agriculture any more. For the thousands of families with agricultural property in India's hinterland, it is difficult to utilize their farmlands simply because their children are no more interested in living in villages. This trend is common all over the country. Villages don't hold any charm any more for the educated younger generation and those who have started living in urban areas.

But an aspiring multi-millionaire should do something different from what others do in order to realize his or her dreams. Or, shall we put it this way: a successful person doesn't do different things, he does things differently.

Doing something new in the field of agriculture undoubtedly offers you a great chance of becoming a multi-millionaire.

For example, if you utilize agricultural land for cultivating herbal and medicinal plants, the income from the yield becomes 10 to 20 times higher than what it is from ordinary farming.

Moreover, as per the Indian Income Tax Act, income from agricultural ventures is exempted from income tax. That means profit and profit, all the way.

Farming of Jatropha plants is another profitable venture. These plants have the capacity to produce oil, similar to petrol. So there is a huge demand for them and many state governments are offering facilities and incentives for cultivating Jatropha.

Herbal and medicinal plants are in great demand, too, not only in India but all over the world. Also, these provide impetus for the traditional Indian healing system of Ayurveda. Thus growing herbs is not just a good thing to do, it can also be a great business proposition.

It's true that there are limitations to buying agricultural land in India. Different Indian states have different restrictions and land ceiling laws. But if you buy land in the names of different members of your family, you can buy a viable-sized lot. The other alternative is to form different companies and buying lands in the name of those companies, adding up to a big chunk of land for cultivation.

The other day I met a businessman who told me that he was cultivating special kind of tomatoes, whose seeds would be sold at a highly lucrative price of ₹1 lakh per kilogram!

At first, I was a bit dubious about his claims. But when I enquired about it further, it became clear that the man was not cultivating tomatoes, but tomato seeds which fetched him a far more attractive price and profits.

You can also consider such seed producing ventures. Flower seed production is globally a big profit making venture. And, now, Indians too are doing well in this area.

Farm land is easily available and at a much cheaper rate, in many foreign countries. Go for such farm land. In the beginning, it might look like a distant dream. But if you want to do something very big, you have to think out of the box and do something new, something beyond the ordinary.

The coming age will be known as the age of bio-technology. So a biotic venture can be a good option for making big successful strides. Herbal products will be in huge demand to counter the use of chemicals in the Pharma industry. You should strike the iron when it is hot. Or, shall I say, an early bird catches the worm. Be that early bird.

There is no denying the fact that people are getting more and more health conscious these days. There is growing concern all over the world about excessive use of chemicals, whether as fertilizers, insecticides or processing agents. Thus, organic farming is one area which is gaining popularity world-wide. As an aspiring multi-millionaire, you may give it a try. The buyers of organic products are well informed and ready to pay more for natural food products. And the market of such products is not limited to India alone; big buying houses world-wide are eager to purchase organic products in bulk.

There are so many innovative ideas in agriculture. Step out of the conventional mould and do something new. No one can then stop you from becoming a multi-millionaire, and sooner than you think!

7

Know More, Earn More

If you are already running a business or venturing into a new one, you should first know what is happening in your particular business segment in your city, in the country, and around the world. You should know as much as you possibly can about your industry. You should also familiarize yourself with the technical progress in that particular field, the demand and supply patterns, the emerging trends — everything. Only then you can think of making big progress, and start making big money on your way to becoming a multi-millionaire.

Whatever area of business you are planning to enter, a thorough and prior knowledge of that field is most beneficial. Rather, it's a must.

For example, there is this well-known magazine published from the United States. It carries hundreds of names of new US manufacturers. This magazine, *Commercial News USA* is circulated free of cost. You can also read it in the American Library, at any of the four metros in India. The easiest way, of course, is to visit the magazine's website, *www.cnewsusa.com*, from the comfort of your office or home. You can then find out details of new manufacturers and their products. Keep yourself updated with the latest knowledge of technology, products and their markets. You may get the inspiration to start something new, something bigger, something better.

Also, make sure to visit the various trade fairs held round the year. The Trade Fair Authority of India and the various chambers of commerce publish the schedules of such fairs much in advance. Visit their websites to find out about the fairs in your trade category. Meet the manufacturers, buyers and suppliers regularly. Explore ever new opportunities to reach higher goals.

To earn more, you should always know more than others do. You should be more knowledgeable about your trade, your industry. You should harness exciting new technology to guide your partners and technicians, to impress your clients and, ultimately, earn much more money, capture bigger markets and higher reputation!

A person who wants to be a multi-millionaire should go beyond his known territory, his city, his state, his country — he must reach out to the world. Only then will he gain that elusive competitive edge over others.

In today's world, the Internet has become indispensable for business growth. You must be Net-savvy to cope with changes in the corporate world, changes in technology and market related activities.

Make it a habit of spending at least half-an-hour daily searching the Net. The world will come closer to you, instantly. You will get to know more and more about the business scenario, business trends, manufacturers, buyers and suppliers in your trade area, in India and in different countries of the world. Who knows, which big opportunity is waiting for you to explore!

The world has become smaller, so has your road to success.

8

Don't Let the Taxman Grab the Lion's Share of Your Millions

To become a multi-millionaire you must have dedication, the tenacity to achieve higher goals, willingness to work hard, and the blessings of your elders. With all these, it will happen very soon.

But make sure that the millions you earn stay yours in the long run. The Income Tax Department should not claim the lion's share.

It's common knowledge that around 30 per cent income from any business goes to the Income Tax Department. Add to it the various surcharges and cess, etc., and the total percentage climbs up to 35 per cent. In other words, out of every 100 rupees of your hard earned money, 35 rupees go to the IT Department.

If you want to be a multi-millionaire, you should find a way to overcome this. But, how?

One very useful way is to start your business in an area of the country where full waiver of income tax is permitted by law. While the income tax rules are the same all over India, but in some states there are exemptions. These are the states which come under the Special Provision Act of Income Tax Laws, where you get exemptions and tax rebates. This not only helps you to garner bigger profit margin and higher cash flow, your wealth also grows at a greater pace. For an aspiring multi-millionaire, it's the most lucrative option available.

In accordance with Article 80IC of Indian Income Tax Act, presently if one sets up an industry in Sikkim, Himachal Pradesh or Uttarakhand, the tax liability on profits becomes negligible, or nearly negligible. Apart from that, the respective state governments also offer lots of facilities for starting industries in these states.

This eventually means that not only are you saving 30 per cent of your income from being taken away as tax, you are also getting a whole lot of facilities and exemptions. Naturally, you get an upper hand over your competitors in the field. But remember that the industry you are setting up in such a state should be a new one. You can't expect tax benefits simply by transplanting your old business venture from another state.

So read Articles 80IC and 80II of the Income Tax Act minutely. Also, do check whether the tax benefit is applicable for 5 years or 10 years, whether there are excise and other tax benefits on raw material, whether you get special benefits if you employ local people, and which sectors are preferred by the respective state government, etc.

Come, get ready for your multi-millionaire journey in tax-favoured pastures.

9

Your Daily Work Schedule is the First Step to Wealth

If you are an aspiring multi-millionaire, it is essential that you make every minute count towards your money-making endeavours. You can't waste any time at all.

In order to make every moment count you must immediately set up a daily work schedule, and then stick to it diligently.

Prepare weekly and monthly schedules, too. Your work schedule will then guide you in your day-to-day activities. It will chart your priorities and the level of importance of various tasks you have to execute whether in a day, a week or a month. When you are aware of the priorities, you are more likely to complete the most important jobs in time and with a fair amount of concentration. Prioritizing jobs will make it easier to execute them faster, better, and in time. Less important jobs can wait and get accomplished in due course.

A successful person must have a work schedule and stick to it. Not only that, all other members of his or her team should also have their respective schedules and execute them diligently.

It's easily understandable that a written work schedule will always help you to keep track of important jobs in hand and to execute them meticulously. Nothing will escape your memory and you will never be caught in an embarrassing or disadvantageous position due to lack of attention and non-execution of the most important jobs.

Multi-millionaires maintain and follow a planned work schedule. In the age of computers, your work schedule can be there at your fingertips and you can suitably alter it at regular intervals. The best option is a laptop computer which is a constant companion of most businessmen these days. You can then make changes and update the schedule, whenever required.

Your time is precious. So, keeping track of how you spend it becomes absolutely necessary. And for the sake of running an organization successfully, you, your managers, workers and everyone should have separate work schedules and execute the same without fail. Work schedules should always be at the top of your agenda.

Never ever let an important job be left unfinished, never miss an appointment.

The Importance of Agenda

If you are a successful businessman, you are, inevitably, a busy person. Your days are apt to be crowded with important engagements, one after another. There would be the usual clash of appointments, dearth of time and, ultimately, avoidable human errors creep in.

Here comes the need of an agenda. This should be your personal agenda, in line with your needs. It's not necessary that to be a master businessman, you should be a memory wizard. With a busy schedule, it's not always possible to remember everything you plan to do. A well charted agenda helps in this situation, keeping you updated and ready — all the time.

You can make a monthly agenda and a weekly one, but a daily agenda helps you to maintain a proper work schedule. Whenever needed, you can change it, alter and adapt it according to your priorities.

Contrary to popular belief, making a daily agenda is easy to do. First, on a piece of paper make a list of all your pending tasks. This will help you make your agenda for the day.

Divide and distribute the daily agenda in three or four parts. Agendas for the morning, lunch hour, afternoon and evening can be scheduled separately. This will help you keep things under control. At the end of the day, objectively assess your achievements and hindrances. And ensure that you always prepare your own agenda, of course with the help of your colleagues and assistants. Don't allow your assistant or manager to make it for you. Let this be a habit with your co-workers too.

A stitch in time saves nine! If you are working without an agenda, despite working hard throughout the day, you may miss the most important tasks. This can be detrimental to your business, sometimes even lead to unrecoverable losses.

Update your daily agenda, sparing some time out of your daily schedule to do so. Allocate jobs to your workers and to yourself, and monitor the whole process everyday. Assess and update without fail. At the same time, make a note of all important meetings in your diary or planner.

Go through your daily agenda more than once in a day. This will help you pre-empt any avoidable slip-ups. Making an agenda is one thing and following it diligently quite another. If you make a daily agenda and forget to review it periodically, the purpose will not be served. In any business, time is the most valuable asset. An agenda makes you master this valuable asset. This is one of the best kept secrets of successful entrepreneurs.

A person who attends his appointments with punctuality and alacrity is always respected. People trust his deeds and words, his reputation grows, and so does his fortune.

10

Put Away Your Ego

A truly successful person never boasts. There are many examples of how bragging killed business fortunes. Self esteem is good, you should always be confident, but unnecessary arrogance should be avoided at any cost. Humility is an essential quality of a successful person in any walk of life.

A successful businessman is also a master in maintaining harmonious social and business relations. Make friends, create a humble image, and make progress.

It's your attitude that attracts people towards you, encourages people to nurture friendly relations with you, and helps you in times of need and, ultimately, smoothens your journey to progress and success.

Believe me, whatever be your achievement or standing in society, brazen pride leads you nowhere. Let people talk about your accomplishment, not the other way around. Never boast.

Our scriptures have repeatedly told us that *Ahamkara* is the root of all evil. People who are humble and never show off, advance better in their business and personal lives. Unnecessary pride shows its adverse results in the long run, and it's a proven fact. So, the best way is to keep yourself busy in your work and never boast of your success.

A friendly attitude goes a long way. Be friendly with your workers, with your business partners, even with your business rivals. The results will be magical. A congenial attitude will encourage an affable business environment and ultimate business growth.

11

Buy Two, Sell One, Keep One

Now I will reveal one of the best kept secrets of the business world — how to achieve maximum benefit by multiplying your profits.

This covert rule of profit making goes like this: "Buy two, sell one, and keep one!"

Initially, it may be a bit of a puzzle to understand this formula of business growth. But actually it's breathtakingly simple once you understand it.

It's as simple as this: when you are buying a house, try to buy, or pay the advance for, two of them. After paying regular instalments for a few months, retain one of them and sell the other one. This will kick-start your financial progress.

This unique formula: Buy two, sell one, and keep one, is really beneficial. Just for a limited period of time you pay instalments for two and acquire one house almost free!

Now, apply the same formula in your business as well.

If you are buying a plot to start your factory or business office, my suggestion is try to buy two plots instead. You will say it's not practical to invest for two plots when you need just one piece of land to build your factory. Believe me, what I've said earlier is a lesser known but an infallible formula. When you sell one plot after some time, you make a substantial profit. And that profit you make without installing another plant or employing additional people.

If you are buying a plot in an area where there is hardly any industry at present, buy an additional adjacent plot. Build your factory on one plot and leave the rest vacant for future use. By the time your factory is built, the price of that surplus land would have escalated. So, if you sell that additional land after sometime you will obviously make a big profit. Thus, you earn a profit even before your factory begins its trial run, which you can use to further grow your business. This is a simple formula but it works incredibly well.

Now, even if you don't sell that surplus land immediately, it will come in handy after sometime when your business is in full swing and you need to expand your business and enlarge your factory. By then, the price of land would have skyrocketed. And here you have prime land, right adjacent to your factory available at no extra investment! You make a profit in such a scenario as well.

Investment in immovable property such as land is always a profitable option in a growing economy like India. The price keeps escalating and there is no looking back. So for anyone who wants to become a multi-millionaire, this is one sure way of making money. Buy land and sell it after sometime, and repeat the process again and again. Even if you don't have enough money to buy surplus land, at least book it straightaway by paying an advance amount and start paying instalments at regular intervals. After sometime, sell it to a suitable buyer. The margin will be enough to make you happier and wealthier.

The profit will be bigger if you buy land in an area where there is no existing commercial activity or development. The moment you start erecting your industrial unit in that area, land price will automatically start rising. And by the time your construction is complete, the price of land in that area would have increased substantially.

It's my earnest suggestion to aspiring multi-millionaire to try and purchase as many vacant plots in and around the plot you are building your industrial unit on. Wait for just two years. By that time your factory would be completed or nearing completion. Sell the surplus land then and you will make a handsome profit.

In my view, this is the surest way of becoming a multi-millionaire in the shortest possible time.

12

Embrace SIP

You may not know much about mutual funds. Perhaps you are unaware of the intricacies of profitable investing. The fact is that, nowadays, people who are not confident about investing in the share market, generally opt for mutual funds.

Yet, you can lose money even in mutual fund investments. So, is there any way out?

Yes there is — and it's called SIP. This is the antidote to painful losses on your investment. Now, what does SIP stand for?

SIP is the acronym for "Systematic Investment Plan". When you plan to invest in a mutual fund, SIP will take care of your profits. It's a foolproof formula for mutual fund investments the world over. Little risk and all gain, that's the SIP assurance.

Let's briefly discuss the functioning of mutual funds before we get to SIP.

Mutual funds operate in various modes. Some mutual funds can be very risky because they invest their entire corpus in the stock market. And you know quite well that uncertainties are a part of this kind of investment. Some mutual funds invest a major part in the stock market and the rest in income securities. Here, too, risk is a considerable factor. The third type of mutual fund is one which invests your money in bonds, precious metals, various securities, etc. Such funds bear comparatively lower risks.

But how does one know which mutual fund is more risky and which one is not. You have surplus money, you want to invest to make a substantial profit and the share market is too volatile! What is the option before you?

Obviously, any investment consultant will tell you to invest a certain amount every month in mutual funds.

Whether you are investing five thousand, ten thousand or fifty thousand rupees in a particular mutual fund or several mutual funds, you must earn profits. If you are guided by SIP in your entire investment procedure, profit is assured.

There are scores of mutual fund companies in the market. Which one is the best? Some of them have the charm of lucrative returns and try to rope in investors on that basis. Others promise instant earnings on a large scale and boast that they alone can provide faster and better returns with the most exciting features.

The investor is lured but not informed properly. The risks and hazards remain either understated or not mentioned at all. Big, impressive pictures of benefits misguide the investor who is puzzled and perplexed.

My suggestion is that you choose the five top and time tested mutual funds. Apply SIP and start investing in them every month. Even if the market is sluggish at any given time, stick to your chosen mutual funds. Naturally, when you stay invested for a longer period, it gives you higher benefits in the long run.

So, the SIP procedure is that you invest in selected mutual funds at regular intervals and keep on doing so in a steady manner. SIP will then ensure that your investment gets a higher percentage and bigger returns. There is every possibility that the mutual funds you're investing in would pave your path comfortably and make you a multi-millionaire.

In the US and many European countries, individual investors always prefer mutual funds over direct share market investments. In fact, small investors are rarely visible in those stock markets, institutional buying takes a major share. But here in India, individual investment in shares is extraordinarily high. But if you are not well versed in share market tactics or you don't have enough time to regularly monitor the share market activity, mutual funds are your best bet. Invest in them and apply SIP. This will not only save you from lots of anxieties but will also bring you better returns.

The biggest benefit of mutual funds is that earnings from them are exempted from income tax. Additionally, if we invest in an equity mutual fund for at least twelve months and sell it thereafter, the gains from such a sale are also absolutely tax-free!

If you are a salaried person or a small entrepreneur and want to invest a moderate amount for higher gains, I will strongly suggest SIP. Invest prudently and diligently in mutual funds and wait for great days ahead!

13

Stick to Your Shares through Volatile and Uncertain Times

People who invest in the stock market know very well that such investments always entail uncertainty. No one can predict accurately whether the price of a particular share price will go up or come down during a day's trading. There are only speculations but no sure answers in the ever fluctuating share market.

Innumerable factors affect the stock market. The daily market movements are essentially driven by sentiment. Often, a major political happening or economic decision completely shakes up the market.

Sometimes, the news of a terror attack on a city or in places of importance cripples the share market. In Mumbai, this has happened on several occasions and the market was completely shut down due to terror attacks. The 26/11 attack was a harsh example. It was centred at the very heart of Mumbai, India's financial capital. The communication revolution added another dimension, bringing a real scene of terror within the four walls of our drawing rooms for forty-eight hours without a break. The share market was the badly affected. This was inevitable. It happened in New

York earlier, in London and elsewhere where there were terror attacks.

A shaky government, the fall of a government, outbreak of a war, each and everything can wobble the sensitive share market. Prices start falling sharply and instantly at such times.

If you want to make money from the share market, or are dreaming of becoming a multi-millionaire, you should not be disheartened or intimidated by such emergency situation or tumultuous developments in the share market. Believe me, this is an advantage in disguise for you. It's often the most opportune moment for entering the market.

I still remember a particular instance when a major mishap doomed the future of a big company. Share prices of the company nosedived overnight. Those who held large numbers of the company's shares were dejected. The share prices reached so low that people were not ready to mention the name of the company in business circles!

Some people, however, took the risk and bought shares at throw-away prices. Within just four years, they hit the jackpot! This is called luck — or whatever you prefer to call it. In fact, such bold decisions can make one a multi-millionaire overnight.

A terrorist attack, the fall of a government, inflation or political turmoil are not ideal situations. But when such calamities do happen, you should not lose your head, or feel threatened. Stand tall in such unpredictable situations and invest as much as you can in the sagging market. This will not only help the country's economy to improve but also pave your path to becoming a multi-millionaire in the long run.

No untowardly incident creates a permanent impact, and hard times never last long. The same also applies to the life cycle of the share market.

Just go through the history of share markets worldwide. Economic slumps, war, natural and political calamities do happen but it's the indomitable human spirit which surpasses all drawbacks and flourishes.

Bad times are not ideal times, but for the fortune seekers they are the most opportune time for investing. Invest in the lean periods and you can reap big profits in the future. This is a reality. A hard earned lesson for all.

But be prepared to stay in the stock market for a longer period. Nothing happens overnight. A short term investment in the market is of no use. Be steady, be determined, and be prepared for a long stint. Don't be distracted by rumours and mere speculations.

The future belongs to those who know how to turn difficulties into opportunities!

14

Learn Face Reading

As a successful businessman, you should learn how to read people's faces while talking to them. Your success is assured once you become competent in face reading. A multi-millionaire must be a master in this art.

What does face reading actually mean? It means perceiving the inner thoughts of the person you are talking to. He may be one of your clients, a buyer or a collaborator, the ability to read his face during face to face interaction will give you an advantage. You will take decisions based on the other person's inner thinking and thus avoid any possible loss to yourself.

For this, first of all you need strong eyesight. Perform some eye exercises regularly every morning for ten minutes at a time. The easiest way is to keep staring at each of your thumbs for five minutes apiece, keeping them in front of your eyes at a distance. Or, early in the morning, keep looking at the rising sun without blinking for a few minutes. Another way is to sit in a dimly-lit room in the yogic lotus pose and keep watching quietly and continuously for 5 to 10 minutes the flame of a lit candle placed in front of you. This will give tremendous power to your eyes and you won't miss even the minute details of anything you are looking at.

Face reading will be easier once you master this yogic practice. A minute observance of the facial movements of the person seated in front of you will guide you to his emotional reactions and responses during the conversation. Once you understand what the other person is thinking, things become easier for you. You start mentally interpreting the emotions and expressions on his face and take your decision in a more pro-active way.

Many people I know face read in their day-to-day business activities and have benefited tremendously from it.

The art of face reading gets perfected with practice. Practice it daily without telling anyone about it. Gradually, you will start noticing the difference. Once you definitely know what the person in front of you is thinking, you can better assess what his next reaction might be. You are then in a very advantageous position in your business deals.

Another important technique in conducting better business deals is to do it in the most peaceful way. Peace should be your disposition whenever you are with people or interacting with people. "Om Shanti Om", this chant should be your constant companion.

Practice meditation daily for 10 to 15 minutes in the early morning hours. This will not only improve your body's metabolism, it will also keep your mind in your complete control. Your looks will get charged with a glow, your mind will be peaceful and in total control and when your face reading ability gets connected to it, no one can then beat you in making business deals.

Believe me, meditation can work miracles! It can bring out the hidden potential in you, making you a powerful and highly controlled person.

The morning is the time when you recharge yourself for the whole day and for facing the world. Use it perfectly by practicing meditation and various eye exercises daily. Soon, you will come to know that you are a changed person. Better health is another boon of daily meditation. And when you have complete control over your mind, nothing is impossible for you.

Once meditation gives you control over your mind, you remain calm and undisturbed. The person talking to you will be impressed by your calmness of mind and controlled expressions.

When you shout, get disturbed and squabble, your business interests suffer. You then never receive what you expect. Neither does it enhance your reputation.

Quarrels, unnecessary arguing, shouting and a rude attitude are a complete no-no for an aspiring multi-millionaire. These kill the very spirit of business. A successful businessman is always polite and friendly. A smiling face always wins, not a frowning one. No ego hassles, no irritation, no high pitched talk — conclude your business deals in the most amicable way. You will then always be in the most advantageous position, always

I know a person who has mastered an unusual habit; he is able to read newspapers upside down. People sitting in front of him and discussing a deal, making random notes on their notepads, making calculations or writing their thoughts were quite unaware that this man was able to read everything!

A person who has business interests abroad, especially in a non-English speaking country, should diligently learn the local language. It will help him to understand what his business associates are discussing among themselves during a meeting. For example, many foreigners who do business with India have some knowledge of Hindi. This helps them to better understand what you are discussing with your Indian partners or colleagues. Small wonder that many Americans and Europeans are learning Chinese these days in order to communicate better with their Chinese business partners. On the other hand, many Chinese, Japanese and Koreans who are doing business in the Gulf have workable knowledge of colloquial Arabic.

These are basic business tricks which are not taught in a business school. But you should know them and apply them and you will become a better businessman, and make a bigger fortune.

15

Never Put All Your Eggs in One Basket

If you aspire to be a multi-millionaire, make sure not to put all your eggs in any one basket.

Thus, never put all your money, resources and energy into a single endeavour. Traditional wisdom dictates that you should stick to your business without any secondary consideration and invest all your money and energy into it. But if you are a big-fortune seeker, you need to think and act differently.

Your resources, money and energy should be spread judiciously. One cannot predict the future. If something untoward happens all of a sudden, you should at least have another option going for you.

Concentrating on a particular business is undoubtedly a good thing but having an alternative business helps in the long run. Right from the very beginning, this should be your policy. It's your safety valve.

If your main business endeavour is facing trouble, the other one can support you by taking care of staff salaries, rent, bank payments, etc. Without a second line of defence, this is simply not possible.

Even those entrepreneurs who have their production units spread out in different parts of the country, should not adhere only to a single industry or business type. They must diversify. Who knows when a critical amendment in government policy, a sudden change in income tax laws, or a massive change in the global market or export policy might jeopardize your business interest overnight.

A careful and watchful entrepreneur always diversifies his business interests. Multiple options bring multiple benefits. And ultimately the decision withstands the test of time, providing much needed succour in times of need.

For day-to-day cash flow and survival of the business and the businessman's own family, a second business becomes indispensable.

Uncertainties are always there. You should accept these as an occupational hazard. You simply don't know when the business you are in suddenly loses its market value, like the nosedive in the IT and BPO businesses post 2008. The financial services and hospitality sectors around the world went into a deep slump in the same period. Sometime a particular product or service loses importance. Sometimes a heavy cancellation of orders in a particular industry cripples a business. So, those who are relying on a single business and put there entire money and energy into just a single enterprise face a big threat to their survival.

A big setback in a solo venture can kill the possibility of your becoming a multi-millionaire. So, make it a point never to put all your money in any one basket, never!

The risk gets lesser when you have more than one business interest, and when all your money and resources are not invested in a single enterprise. This prudent exercise will help you absorb the shock of a sudden mishap to a great extent. Setback in one of the businesses can be stabilized by the others.

Run your business enthusiastically and effectively, but keep an auxiliary business at hand — always.

This will be a huge advantage in the long run.

16

Keep Your Business Funds Away from the Stock Market

If you want to be a multi-millionaire, my advice is to keep your business funds out of the stock market. It may sound a bit odd but it is true.

I still remember what one of the most successful US industrialists once said: "If you are an industrialist and your industry is running well, you should not invest in the stock market."

At first I could not understand the real meaning of his words. After all, people invest in the share market to earn more money. If an industrialist has surplus money, he will naturally put it into the stock market. How can this jeopardize one's business interests?

But, later, when I reflected some more on what the industrialist had said, it dawned on me that he had quite valid reasons.

The share market runs on a different logic altogether, entirely different from the way a business is run. According to this American businessman, let us suppose an industrialist buys a lot of shares from his business funds and makes a lot of profit when share prices rise substantially. Obviuosly, he will be very happy with his profits but herein lies the trap. What he has earned through the share market required no production or industrial activity but simply a bullish rise in the overall market — and that's transitory. But the profits may distract him from his business activities and he may start investing more and more in shares, rather than concentrate on his industry. This will be an unwise decision on his part. The share market never remains the same. It always goes through ups and downs which will disturb both his concentration and the funds needed for his business. If his company's money is invested in shares, his attention in the share market's ups and downs will not be a one day affair. It will become a regular feature and that's going to affect his existing business prospects severely. And if the market falls flat on its face, the future of his business will also be put in jeopardy.

It's not a taboo but a prudent decision for an aspiring multi-millionaire to steer clear of putting his business funds in the share market. He should focus on his industry, his business prospects and growth. And that's a full time affair.

This is not to say that an industrialist can't make money by investing his personal savings in the share market. Of course, he can. But then he has to concentrate his time and energy in the trading of shares; read newspapers, watch television, discuss with share market pundits, keep a watch on various economic, corporate and political decisions and happenings, only then will he become a master investor. But this needs time and tenacity. Does an industrialist have that time and energy to divert from his mainstream business interests? Surely not.

My suggestion, therefore, is that unless and until you are sure that you have enough spare time and energy, don't get into the day-to-day affairs of the share market. Better invest your personal funds in mutual funds, it's a balanced way — and hassle free too.

In the last forty years of my professional life, I have seen many industrialists go bankrupt due to their overexposure in the stock market. They invested the money meant for their own business in stocks. They took loans, even mortgaged their factories, speculating for a windfall. They wanted to get rich overnight. But when the jolt came from the ever fluctuating share market, it was too late. Their industry was gone.

If you aspire to be a multi-millionaire, don't put your business venture's funds in the stock market.

17

Write Down Your Life's Goals

You don't have much money, you are hard working, you are committed to your job, your thinking is in the right direction and your intention is good. Now it's time to sit down and put down on a piece of paper the ultimate goal of your life.

To become a multi-millionaire, you have to dream big. And in order to turn your big dream into reality you need to introspect and assess your strengths.

Take out some time, two to three hours at least, ideally on a holiday. Don't let anyone, even your family members, disturb you. Switch off your mobile phone. Think intensively and deeply and write down the goals and motives of your life, for the next five, ten or twenty years.

Anyone who wants to earn millions and billions must have his goals decided and defined for the years to come. The profession you are in, its progress and prospects should be critically analyzed and assessed. Only then can you fulfil the goals of your life.

The most important thing is to introspect and put down in writing the goals of your life. Once that is done, you'll be in a better position to steer your life and future activities. Your life map you draw up should be read and reviewed once a month. I have personally assisted many people to identify and write down the goals of their lives.

The process we followed is quite simple. The person had to take leave from his office and both of us would meet at some place other than our homes or offices, usually in a room in a comfortable hotel where no one would disturb us. I would then tell the person to sit by himself and write down the goals of his life, one by one. Within an hour or so, he would come up with an initial list.

We would then discuss the list exhaustively, a process which would take several hours. Typically, some goals in the initial list would be vague, some would not have been thought out properly, and some goals which the person had in mind would not have been written down at all. I would then suggest, "Please take your time, there's no hurry, think it over and then pen down each and every goal. Keep in mind that this is going to guide and, ultimately, change your life and bring you success."

After a break for lunch, we would get back to the task again. It would take many more hours, but by the evening, and after a lot of corrections, additions and deletions, the final list would be ready.

We would then discuss each and every item on the list minutely once again. After this long discussion and deliberation, the guide map of the person's life for the next 20 to 30 years would come to light. When both of us were satisfied, the draft was finalized.

If you want to be highly successful and dream of becoming a multi-millionaire, or want to make it big in any field of your choice, you must put down your life goals in writing. This is not a 10- or 15-minute job; it will more likely take a whole day, and it must cover every aspect of your life.

The human life is a rare gift to us. We must have the will to reach the top of whatever we are doing. We must have dreams to earn big and get bigger recognition. You are ready to work hard to realize your dreams, and you are steady and consistent in your work, but a roadmap, a map where the next ten, twenty or thirty years of your life are defined and charted, will greatly help you attain your goals.

If the draft is well documented, it will undoubtedly guide you to bigger success.

When drafting the list of your goals, you should introspect and evaluate every point. It's your life, so there should be no interference in the process.

Once it is finalized, you can discuss it with your spouse, close friends and your colleagues. You can accept their genuine suggestions, make minor changes here and there, but it remains your guidebook for life, penned by you.

And, believe me; once you are ready with such a guide map, it will definitely change your life.

18

Secrets of a Stress-Free Life

If you want to be constantly at the peak of your productivity, you must be free of tension. This should be at the top of your agenda if you want to be highly successful.

Tension, which is a bane of our modern lifestyle, hampers not only our business interests but also our personal lives. To be successful, you must make it a habit to be tension-free.

Typically, a successful businessman's life is full of stress and tension. But, it need not be so. In reality, it's not necessary that you should be under stress in order to be successful. A stress-free life makes your business more productive, more innovative and more prosperous.

Only when you are free of stress are you in the most ideal situation to run a business perfectly. When your mind is calm and relaxed, you can take better decisions, solve problems more decisively, and plan new ventures to accelerate your progress.

Once rid of stress, you will no longer be anxious, you will look and feel younger and will generally be more enthusiastic and agile. The glow in your face will emit positivist. Your life will be healthier, happier and busier.

If you make it a point to not fall prey to anxieties, there is every possibility that you will soon become free of tensions. As the *Bhagavad Gita* says, you should do your duty diligently but shouldn't get emotionally attached to it and neither should you pin all your hopes upon the outcome you expect from your pursuits. This is the key to an emotionally healthy and tension-free life.

World renowned Canadian Doctor Sir William Osier has aptly said that tension has become a part of our lives and most of our diseases are directly related to tension.

It's a warning bell for businessmen who are anxious all the time. Anxiety can cripple us and, ultimately, make us sick. Surely, an ailing person can't be an ideal flag-bearer of a successful enterprise.

The Indian tradition provides us all the ingredients for a tension-free life. Simplicity, sincerity, hard work and a serene spirituality encompass all the required antidotes to anxieties and apprehensions. Remember what Lord Krishna has said in the immortal *Bhagavad Gita:* "Leave your anxieties to the Supreme Being, carry out your duties — forget everything else!"

If you can follow this principle in your life, anxieties and related illnesses will soon be a thing of the past.

A tense businessman is always disturbed, peeved. A small provocation and he starts shouting at his assistants, workers, suppliers, mechanics, his own family members — virtually everyone. A tension-fed lifestyle takes you nowhere, certainly no nearer to your dreams. Tension is a waste of energy, a waste of time. Why should you carry the unnecessary burden of tension in your life? Behaving erratically and aggressively is not the solution for getting rid of tension. Rather, it aggravates your mental strife and rest lessens. This ultimately harms your business interest. It's not productive or encouraging in any manner.

A strong will-power-can drive out tension from your life forever. Make a promise to yourself that you would rather go hungry than let tension bother you again. If you are determined, you can turn away all tensions from your life.

Be relaxed, be peaceful. Let your colleagues also be likewise. Conduct your business at ease — and prosper.

19

Avoid Altercations

If you want to be a successful multi-millionaire, follow this basic mantra — never argue with anyone.

Based on my experience I firmly believe that if you take this mantra seriously, it will ultimately help you in earning multi-millions. If you are egoistic or quarrelsome by habit, my earnest request is that you shun the habit immediately for the sake of success in your endeavours.

In any business, the customer is the undisputed king. If you believe this with sincerity, you will see within a few days that you are a changed person. Your habits of argument will subside substantially. Your business reputation will soar. So will your business prospects.

People who come in contact with you will remember your amicable and understanding nature. This will undoubtedly be an asset for your business.

Even in personal life, quarrelling with one's spouse, children or parents takes one nowhere. In every quarrel while one person wins the other one loses.

What does one get out of it? Just ego satisfaction! So, never fall into the trap. Never argue again.

Of course, it does not mean that you should not put forward your opinion firmly in any discussion. But do so in a professional and courteous way, without any outburst of temper. Don't become adamant. For a temporary satisfaction of your ego, you will lose everything; a good relationship, a long lasting friendship, or a growing business alliance. The chasm thus created in a moment often lasts a lifetime.

You have your own views about an issue; obviously, the other person also has his or her own views and thoughts. Both of you can discuss the issues agreeably and come to a conclusion. Don't stress just your own perspective, that will not give you a mutually amicable solution.

Arguing for the sake of your ego satisfaction is an unnecessary waste of time and energy. Shun this habit. It leads to unnecessary tension and will earn you a lot of enemies. Better be polite, amicable and understanding. It will give you peace of mind, earn you goodwill and friends, and ultimately help you in growing your business. Your personality should be such that whoever meets you finds you a pleasure to be with.

20

Don't Expect Others to Make You Rich

If you want to prosper in business and in your life, learn to be self-sufficient, confident and cool. And, don't have expectations from others.

Most of us think that if we are in business, we need help from others. This is a fallacy. In fact, this false idea often becomes the root cause of our misery.

When you expect something from another person and your expectation is not fulfilled, you feel dejected and lose your enthusiasm. It perturbs you for days on end and hampers your actions to a great extent. So, it's always better to not expect anything from anyone.

If you are committed to making progress in your endeavours, never rely or depend on others for the outcome. Be self-reliant, do it yourself, and wait for the best. Forget about earning praise or accolade from others.

The ancient wisdom from the *Rig Veda* and the *Yoga Sutra* teaches us the same thing: you are the sole designer of your fate and fortune, no one else. The onus rests entirely on you. No other person can ever decide your future.

Apply this cardinal policy in your business realm and in your personal life to achieve exemplary success and earn millions.

Dependence on others for your personal success is a false crutch that brings no constructive result. You can't be a successful businessman by relying on others to deliver your success.

In fact, a setback in your business is likely when you become over reliant on others. Be it your colleagues or business partners, if your exaggerated expectations are not fulfilled, you will feel mentally disturbed, let down and helpless. Don't let this happen, it's not going to help you in any manner.

Often we see in business circles that the business community helps each other in moments of need. It's normal human practice to stand by each other in times of distress. This is humanity and a noble thing, no doubt. But the problem arises when we become dependent on others and expect help from them as a matter of routine, almost as a matter of right.

Suppose you have helped one of your fellow businessmen with monetary assistance which helped him ward off an unexpected distress or disaster. He would, naturally, be grateful, but don't expect similar help from him as a matter of right if perchance you are in distress in the future and urgently need money. Believing that your friend will surely help you may turn out to be a false belief.

You may find that the same friend you helped years back is quite evasive and non-committal about your request. What will happen then? You will be in for a mental shock. You will lose trust in people, you will curse all friendships and suffer from severe mental distress for a long time.

Avoid such situations. If possible, help others in their hour of need but don't expect the same from them. Be clear in your conscience. Be relaxed and cool. Be happy.

21

Your Business Growth Depends on Your Cash Flow

For a successful businessman and an aspiring multi-millionaire, nothing is more essential than regular and dependable cash flow. In fact, more than anything else a serious disruption in cash flow can virtually cripple a business or industry. It can prove fatal, turning a business venture into a blind alley, jeopardizing its growth and future prospects.

In the matter of cash flow, you must always be on your guard and take pre-emptive measures. For one, always maintain cash reserves to cover at least two months of your cash expenses.

Cash flow is the life line of any business. You have expenditures on a regular basis to keep your business running. Expenditure on raw materials, manpower, infrastructure, taxes, rent, interest on bank loans — the list is endless. But if the cash you were expecting does not arrive in time due to one reason or another, or if you make an unexpected loss in some business deal, what will you do? Without a cash reserve, you will find yourself in difficulty, which can turn all your plans topsy-turvy and leave you feeling helpless.

People you owe money to won't be satisfied with your problems or alibis. They would want their money in time, not excuses. Equally, healthy long-term business relations depend on timely payments. Your reputation is also at stake, so is your creditworthiness. The biggest casualty of all is your confidence. Whatever business you are in, your cash flow must be intact.

You must, therefore, learn to manage your cash flow properly. Generally, making a list of weekly cash flow helps. But in a small enterprise, a ready-reckoner of monthly cash flow is also advisable. Such a cash flow chart will keep you informed about how much money you are likely to receive that week, that fortnight or that month, and what your various expenditures are. This will help you to avoid any embarrassment or difficulties when facing your creditors or employees.

A successful businessman makes prior arrangements for an emergency fund to be available in the time of need. In hard times, when the cash flow is disrupted all of a sudden, this contingency fund helps one to keep up the pace and save one's business from downfall and one's reputation intact.

A setback due to a disruption in cash flow saps the momentum of a business. Even business relationships are affected. And it's a universal fact that business fortune depends heavily on relationships and one's reputation in the market. Keep this in mind and never let problematic cash flow jeopardize your future.

One way of tackling emergency cash flow situations is by maintaining a fixed deposit account in a bank. You can then avail overdraft against the fixed deposit in times of need. This is a most ideal arrangement for keeping cash flow problem at bay.

There are also other time tested methods to cope with cash flow emergencies. One is to sell some goods or assets to arrange for cash. The other is to take help of the savings of your spouse or close family members in the hours of need. One can also take loans from family members and friends to overcome severe cash flow problem. These are the solutions that will not only help you in an emergency, they will relieve you from anxiety and agonies and you will find that proper arrangement for an undisturbed cash flow keeps your business in good health and ever-growing.

Credit-worthiness is the main casualty of disturbed cash flow. Once you lose it, it's not easy to recover. The result is your trust-worthiness is lost, you don't get service and goods at preferential prices and you end up paying more for them. No one is ready to extend your credit limit. It's one of the biggest setbacks of business life.

So, if you are dreaming high, looking to becoming a multi-millionaire — let there be a healthy cash flow and contingency fund available for any emergency.

Always remember, your business growth is directly related to your cash flow.

22

Thinking of Evading Taxes? Don't!

There are several kinds of taxes applicable on business profits and earnings. For the sake of running your business successfully and earning consistent profits, it's necessary that you should always make a proper assessment of payable taxes and pay them regularly. Never steal taxes. It never helps

Whether it's income tax, sales tax or excise duty, any misappropriation or evasion will bring serious consequences.

If you are planning to be a multi-millionaire, take a pledge today that you will never evade taxes in any situation. The grave consequences of tax fraud are many, imprisonment being one of them. Going to jail is hardly a good option; it can destroy your business reputation and make future progress difficult. Beware of such an outcome and be honest about paying your taxes.

Of course, there are many provisions whereby you can save taxes legally, but if you try doing so illegally you should be ready to face the music.

For example, if you set up an industry in Himachal Pradesh, you get a lot of tax benefits, including exemptions in income tax.

Many other states also offer different tax benefits and tax holidays. Saving tax in such a manner is perfectly within the legal parameters and it's also beneficial all round. But fudging taxes with doctored accounts and false documents will always be a punishable offence. Heavy fines, imprisonment, black listing of the firm, anything can happen. This is not an ideal situation for an entrepreneur who has big future dreams.

Concentrate on growing your business and profits, not on evading tax. Income tax law is harsh on frauds, both in India and all over the world. Any good tax planner can show you legal ways and means of substantial tax saving. That should be the limit of tax planning.

Remember, an honest mind is responsible and productive. It ensures a healthy environment for ultimate business growth.

23

Assess Your Assets

Once you are on your way to becoming a multi-millionaire, you'll have a lot of property. While your staff will look after the day to day activities of maintaining them, personal asset assessment at regular intervals is also necessary.

Physical asset verification (PAV) is a very important part of business. Documents, statements, print-outs are all well and good but PAV is essential. At regular intervals, you yourself, or a member of your family, should physically inspect all your properties and also thoroughly check their documents. This small step will save you from a lot of problems and complications.

Thus, check your financial assets which may be in the form of shares, bonds and fixed deposits and tally them with their documents that you possess. Check the creditors and debtors lists, and any recent purchases related to your business. Whether a property is old or new — everything should be reviewed at regular intervals.

This will not only update you with your assets, it will also reveal if there are any irregularities or flaws in your records.

Also, a regular inspection of the properties and financial assets you have makes you aware of those which are profitable and those which may be languishing, which ones you can sell to make substantial profit and which ones you should get rid off to avoid any further loss.

This procedure of physical asset verification helps you in more than one way, keeping your financial activities progressive and profitable.

24

Don't Ever Get Depressed

As you progress in your business or your way to becoming a multi-millionaire, your workload increases, and so do your daily anxieties and uncertainties. There are setbacks and losses, a lack of leisure activities and loss of regular contact with friends and family members. An unwanted guest then tries to enter your life! Be careful of this unwanted guest; never ever allow depression to get to you. A depressed person simply can't be a successful person.

You should do your work energetically and enthusiastically because depression can easily choke your progress by upsetting your judgment and decision-making ability.

A depressed person has many physical symptoms: the throat dries up, you experience excessive perspiration, trembling of hands, digestive problems and lack of sleep. Overall, a depressed person is always tense and disturbed. A disturbed person can't be expected to deliver the best results in any sphere.

Setbacks and losses are a part of every business. Treat these as a passing phase. Don't get depressed by temporary setbacks. There is no point in thinking negatively, no point in thinking that the entire world is a hopeless place or that nothing good will ever happen to you.

Be firm, be positive, be enthusiastic in your thoughts and actions.

The Greek philosopher and immortal mathematician Pythagoras told us 2,600 years back: "Concern should drive us into action and not into a depression. No man is free who cannot control himself."

The same is applicable today in our daily life.

Hindu scriptures also exhort us to always work diligently and leave everything else to God. What is happening today and what will happen tomorrow are destined by God. So, where is the point in getting disheartened? We should work for our betterment and progress, undisturbed by any situation. This is the only way to reach your ultimate goal.

Yes, medical treatment is available for chronic depression. You can consult a clinical psychologist for treatment. But it is not required in most cases, unless it's a situation of deep mental shock or insanity.

Depression is usually a problem of wrong thinking. It can be cured by applying your mind in a very positive way. According to psychologists, our mind is a super storehouse of power. We can do anything we wish to, if we apply our mental energy in a proper way. Depression and phobia are the results of a negative thought pattern, which can be altered by applying strong will-power in the positive direction.

Start thinking positively, see everything around you from a positive angle, take responsibility for your actions and drive away any negative thought immediately. Very soon, you will be a changed person — confident, enthusiastic and ever-inspired!

In moments of depression, remember your good days, your achievements, the happier moments of your life. Think of your achievements in school and college, the time when you secured your first order ousting tough business competition, when your company or you earned awards, or any happy memory connected with your children — anything. Write down those moments and remember them whenever you feel low. This will work as an antidote to depression.

Assess your most positive qualities. Everyone has his or her special qualities which differentiates them from all others. In God's plan for the universe, everyone has a place.

Just concentrating on negative thoughts doesn't help you in any way. Rather, it will aggravate the situation. Better take control of your life and your thoughts and march towards your own progress.

Lack of sleep, lack of concentration, irritation — these are the common symptoms of a depressed mind. Getting dependent on medicines won't help either. You yourself hold the key. Change your thought pattern and the situation will change straightaway. Everything will soon be perfect once again.

Always aim for the best in everything and work constantly to achieve the highest standard in your life and work. Depression arises when you leave tasks mid-stream, when you don't fulfil your goals, or when you go through a major economic crisis. One example would be when your payments are stuck but there is a whole list of creditors demanding their dues.

Don't lose heart at such time; that won't help. Instead, try to solve the problem in the most pragmatic manner. Write down all the problems you're facing and then try to find their solutions, one by one. If you are running a business, you must be prepared for any untoward situation. Remember, too, that such a phase is temporary and will pass away soon. At such times, you must think about your long term stakes in the market, the reputation of your company, its goodwill and its future. Also, your entire staff looks to you for leadership. Depression is not going to help you. You have to be pro-active and courageous in overcoming an adverse situation. God helps him who helps himself. You have to be your own guide and philosopher. Believe me, no situation is everlasting and there is a way out for every problem.

Recently, I was in Pune taking part in a symposium. A young man came to me and asked, "Sir, what would you do if you are depressed yourself?" I smiled at him and said, "Quite simple! I'll do the same thing that I'm advising you to do".

So, this is not mere sermonizing, it's my conviction.

Let me elaborate further. In my moments of depression I remember inspiring moments from my life. I think of my achievements rather than burdening myself with negative thoughts.

I remember some days of my youth. I remember when in the 1970s I was chosen the Best Youth Representative from India by Lions International. I was consequently invited to the International Youth Council Meet in USA. Every expense, air tickets to and fro, hotel accommodation, etc., everything was arranged by Lions International.

Or that day when I had completed my unique practical course on taxes: "Zero to Hero". Today, after twenty-five years it's still popular. Thousands of people have benefited from it.

I think of the day when I started my popular TV show, "Tax Guru". Now wherever I go, whoever I meet at the airport, at the railway station, at the market place, even in hospitals, people eagerly enquire about my programme, and tell me how much they have benefited from it. It's an achievement for me.

In 2008, in the months of January and February, I travelled all over India with CNBC-Awaaz TV channel to spread my "Reduce Tax" movement. I took the movement to every corner of India. In full view of the media, I met thousands of taxpayers in small and big cities of India who took my movement further.

On 28 February 2008, the Honourable Finance Minister submitted the budget in the Parliament. To our very pleasant surprise we discovered that our India-wide movement had brought tremendous success. The Finance Minister had not only brought down the tax rate, he also announced various tax benefits. Our demand was thus ultimately met.

In this manner, when I start thinking of my achievements one by one, the very idea of depression flies out of the window!

Don't get into the depression trap. Never wallow in negative thinking. Think positively, and look for the positive side of any situation. A fearful, apprehensive mind is also a sign of depression. Be fearless. Face every situation with responsibility and authority. Then you will not suffer from fear.

When you are confident and affirmative in your thoughts, no one can stop your progress. Your business and fortune will definitely grow.

Everything starts from your mind. Your mind is the most valuable asset you have. You get all your mental energy and thoughts from this endless resource. Use it wisely and effectively. Get the best out of it. You can solve all your problems by positive thinking. In this way, you will find a solution to each and every problem of your business and life.

If you use your mind positively and effectively, it will lead you to progress and financial fortune. Decision making, taking action, assessing, reassessing, evaluating and improving . . . every aspect of your business is guided by your thoughts. So, thoughts are all-powerful. Point them in the right direction. This is the secret of financial or any other kind of success.

Be fearless, this is the key. God is your saviour.

Swami Vivekananda said: "The whole secret of existence is to have no fear. Never fear what will become of you, depend on no one. The moment you reject all help, you are free."

In Madras (now Chennai), more than a hundred years ago Swami Vivekananda uttered these most inspiring words: "Stand up, be bold, be strong. Take the whole responsibility on your own shoulders, and know that you are the creator of your own destiny. All the strength and succour you want is within yourself. Make your own future."

This is the basic philosophy of every successful life. Whatever help, whatever power you're seeking, all is within you. It's you and you alone who can make the difference in your life. It all depends on the way you think and act.

Swami Vivekananda told us of self reliance and of becoming responsible: "Why are people so afraid? The answer is that they have made themselves helpless and dependent on others. We do not want to do anything ourselves. We want a Personal God, a Saviour or a Prophet to do everything for us."

Take a vow. From now on, don't be dependant on others. It's totally unnecessary. The necessary thing is you should be self reliant, fearless in all your actions and positive in your attitude and thinking. Once you make yourself that strong, every problem will look insignificant to you. This is a proven formula.

Exercise regularly, meditate, keep your body and mind fit. Make your life, your activities and, of course, your business most successful. The whole world is there in front of you. Conquer it!

25

Don't Treat Your Body Like a Junkyard

As your business grows and your wealth flourishes manifold, you start frequenting business functions and parties where there is a lot of food to eat and plenty to drink. But always keep in this mind while attending such parties and business meets — never let your body become the wholesale dumping ground of a variety of food.

Next to your mind, your body is your most precious asset. It's unique, it's most complex yet perfectly and variedly functional. Your capacity for action, whether in business or in your personal life, depends directly on your body. A healthy and fit body assures a fit attitude and agility in life. You need to take care of your body's health to ensure a healthy and wealthy disposition of your business.

Indian business neighbourhoods are full of *chaat* shops, spicy food joints, *mithai* outlets where *ghee* is lavishly used, cold drink kiosks and the ubiquitous tea and coffee vendors. I've seen business friends surviving the whole work day on such food. Intake of junk food, tea and coffee, cold drinks, etc. is so frequent that there is hardly any discipline or routine adhered to for meals. Ultimately, the result shows in ill-health!

Not just that. The spicy and junk food eating business community is also so fond of *Paan* and *Gutka* that it has reached the level of addiction.

Healthy food habit is an idea which most Indian business people seem quite unaware of. In Western countries, people in business are very health conscious. They exercise regularly, jog, take enough fruit and milk (mostly fatless or skimmed) and milk products, green vegetables, sprouts, etc. to maintain their health and energy.

Traditionally, Indian food habits are divided into several categories. *Satvik* food is best for health. *Rajsik* food can be taken occasionally, *Tamasik* food never! Take lots of fruit in your food, drink milk, and, of course, eat at regular times, without missing a meal. There shouldn't be a big gap between two meals, and avoid junk food and frequent tea and coffee. If you are determined to take a big leap forward in your business, keep yourself fit as a fiddle. Success begins not just at home but with your food habits, too.

A disciplined and controlled lifestyle is the key to a fit body. There should be a fixed time for breakfast, lunch and dinner. The British even have fixed tea hours. This helps you to keep control over your health and monitor your lifestyle. An erratic, indisciplined lifestyle will come in the way of your flight to progress.

Quit smoking. Smoking can lead to a whole range of ailments, from chest infection, tuberculosis to cancer. Alcohol is another culprit behind the deteriorating health of many. Get rid of anxieties and insomnia. Go to bed every night at a fixed time, don't become a midnight owl. Early to bed and early to rise — the good old proverb is valid even in modern times.

I am not suggesting that you live like a hermit but a balanced and healthy lifestyle keeps your body and mind perfectly tuned and charged with natural freshness and health. Your body looking like a granary bursting at the seams is not a healthy or pleasant sight.

Another suggestion, and one which may appear be a bit baffling at first; keep silent for a least one day every month. In the Indian tradition this is called *Maun Vrat* and it has long-lasting benefits.

Mahatma Gandhi used to maintain *Maun* (silence) every Monday. Among his close circle, Monday was therefore known as *Maun Diwas*! Even if a VIP or foreign dignitary came to meet him on any Monday, Gandhiji would express himself only in writing. Speaking was not allowed on that day in his Ashram. And the Mahatma, as you know, was the most disciplined and dedicated person of his generation.

A businessman might protest, "My entire business and all my business deals are based on verbal communications. How can I remain silent for the whole day?"

But if you make it a practice, people will come to know about it and respect your choice. They will make special arrangement for that one day in the month. And in today's world, e-mail, SMS, written letters, fax can handle all your business communication and deals.

Keeping silent *(Maun)* will help you to introspect, initiate dialogue with your inner self and help you solve many of your problems as you silently ponder over them. Just as a fast purifies your inner system and fortifies your immunity, *Maun* does the same for your mind, making it clutter free and fortifying it.

26

Profit from Property through the New UTI — "United To Invest"

In business and investment circles UTI means, Unit Trust of India. But here I'm talking about a new UTI which means "United to Invest". This brand new idea can emerge as a popular investment option in the real estate sector.

This unique way of investment will particularly help smaller investors. In fact, it will encourage individual investors with small and medium budgets to invest in property and real estate in a bigger way.

This investor friendly way will not only bring fresh life in the burgeoning real estate business, it will build new avenues for individual investors to profit from property UTI facilitates small-budget investors to invest jointly, with each one investing 10 to 15 per cent of the total funds required.

The most important task in this method is that of bringing together like-minded people and convincing them to invest in real estate. For better returns from UTI in the real estate sector, the minimum investment corpus should be ₹1 crore for a metro city and ₹50 lakh for any other major city. A group should constitute of 8-15 people. Try to avoid creating a group of more than fifteen people lest it become too unwieldy.

First, a group leader or "fund manager" has to be appointed from among the team members. A fund manager's prime responsibility is to manage the fund usefully and scout for profitable investment opportunities. At the very beginning, the fund manager's scope, terms and the time limit of his assignment should be laid down.

The next important step is the group's agreement about investing in real estate. Such a consensus as a collective body is a must. The UTI group's legal status or constitution could be a corporate unit or a partnership firm. The fund manager makes a clear assessment of the scopes and facilities available and tax liabilities of the group as well as of every member of the group. He makes various suggestions and gives advice, from time to time.

United to Invest (UTI) is a new concept in investment that works in much the same way as an organized mutual fund. It believes in the Walt Disney maxim: If you are a dreamer, realize it now!

There is opportunity of regular and substantial profitable investment by small and big investors in India's growing property market. This opportunity is available both in the small and big Indian cities alike. For this, you just need a group of like-minded and honest people who all want to make big profits in the property market, and are willing to do so, collectively.

Members of UTI groups get preferential treatment in the highly profitable property market. For an individual client, the builder or developer may offer only a nominal discount, but a group enjoys substantial negotiating power for higher discounts.

It's common sense that if instead of a single flat you intend to buy ten, twelve or fifteen flats together, the builder will scale down the price of each unit and also provide various other benefits, like pre-launch booking benefit, cash payment benefit, friendship benefit, etc.

UTI type of investment can also be a major profit making option in buying agricultural plots, which the buyers can either resell or develop into better properties. Another option is to buy flats and rent them out. I know of an NRI who has bought almost 10,000 flats in India, which he now rents out. By this, he earns millions every month.

In the coming years, UTI type of investment pattern will become popular in India. It offers an avenue to small investors to think big. Builders and developers also find it highly beneficial, because it brings bulk money into circulation to boost up the market. For the investors, UTI gives the unique power to bargain and compel the builder or developer to scale down the prices and offer extra benefits.

You can also apply the UTI principle in other business domains to achieve higher growth. Reaching the pinnacle of profits without high investment is possible through this unique method.

If you are getting a big order, a big tender or a big project which is beyond your financial capacity, try to accomplish it by applying the policy of UTI. Create a group of like-minded investors and realize your big dreams. It will bring you closer to your goal of becoming a multi-millionaire.

27

Enthusiasm is the Key

Once you have decided that you want to become a multi-millionaire, there should be no looking back. Stick to your goal without any distractions and keep making steady progress towards its achievement.

Enthusiasm plays a key role in every journey of our life. When your business is small and your expectations are big, often you will find yourself discouraged from time to time. But if you keep your spirits high and never let despair and discouragement get near you, you will undoubtedly succeed in your endeavour. There are numerous instances of people from humble backgrounds who rose to the pinnacle of power by virtue of their confidence, perseverance, hard work and, above all, limitless enthusiasm.

Founder Chairman of Infosys, N. R. Narayana Murthy addressed the students of New York University in 2007. In the course of his talk, he told them that once he had to starve for 108 hours at a stretch because he had no money. But in the same speech he also mentioned that despite facing a lot of hardships abroad, he never got distracted from his goal of creating a world class enterprise. What guided him in reaching his goal was not just money — he started out with only ₹25,000 — or help from his friends, but his never-ending enthusiasm.

Truly, if you are guided by enthusiasm, no power in this world can stop you from reaching your goal. If you are ever enthusiastic in all your actions and never boast about your achievements, you are bound to grow in your business by leaps and bounds.

In Ramnad (Ramanathapuram), Swami Vivekananda said:

> "The Vedanta recognizes no sin; it only recognizes error. And the greatest error, says Vedanta, is to say that you are weak, that you are a sinner, a miserable creature, and that you have no power and you cannot do this and that."

The greatest achievers in life and business never lack enthusiasm. Temporary setbacks and losses are a part of every journey. Work for the betterment and growth of your business and never get disheartened by any untoward incident or outcome. Trust in yourself and your ability — you'll then overcome all obstacles that come your way.

Swamiji had said: "You have to grow from the inside out. No one else can teach you. There is no other teacher but your own soul."

There are so many inspirational writings by thinkers, psychologists, saints, personality trainers and achievers. Read them, be inspired and guided by them to move up the ladder of achievement.

Whenever despair or a sense of defeat gathers within you, think about God. God is your shepherd. If you are candid and committed to your intentions, success will never elude you.

Whatever power you are seeking is well within you. Just bring out that power to face the world, face all difficult situations — no problem will then be too big for you to solve.

Once you have made up your mind to achieve success, you then have a clear goal to achieve. Never forget for a moment what you need to do, where you have to go. Your life's direction will get defined by your goal. Like the Indian tradition of reading the *Gita* every morning for one's daily inspiration, you should always remember and remain enthusiastic about your goal.

"Fill the brain with high thoughts, highest ideals, place them day and night before you, and out of that will come great work," said Swami Vivekananda.

Read the biographies of great statesmen, scientists and industrialists and see how they faced both adversaries and adversities and ultimately won. A winner never quits and a quitter never wins, this is a vital secret of success.

You must have heard of Thomas Alva Edison, the great American scientific inventor, who held the greatest number of patents in his name. He faced seemingly hopeless situations and failures so many times but he never abandoned his research. Some of the greatest inventions of humankind would never have seen the light of day had Edison ever quit in despair.

Think about it, the greatest of recessions don't discourage great industrialists. The Tata empire grew manifold worldwide even in the difficult first decade of the 21st century, so have the Mittals. In fact, they have made the best of adverse times and triumphed.

28

Divide Your Day into Perfect Quarters

You must have heard of Breakdance; now how about breaking up your daily work schedule into several parts? I've tried doing this and have found the practice extremely helpful.

Write down your daily tasks on a piece of paper and prioritise them according to their importance. Once you are able to prioritise them successfully, and execute them accordingly, you will find that your life has become more manageable and fruitful. Also, you will be able to spend quality time on your work, with yourself, and with your family. Finding time for everything will become easy.

Being a workaholic is fine; it may even be necessary at times for making progress in your business endeavours. But your work should occupy only an allotted amount of time span every day, nothing beyond that. You have other important aspects in your life besides making a fortune. Your business is of prime consideration no doubt, but there is your health, your hobbies, your family, your social activities, acquiring further knowledge, time to unwind — the list is long. You can't sacrifice any one of these for the other.

So, make a chart right now. We can call it the 25% chart. Your business or professional activities should occupy just 25 per cent of the time. Yes, the first 25 per cent area of the chart must be allotted to your business and related activities.

The next 25 per cent space should be allotted to your self-development. Keep on developing yourself for the future. Learn new things, new technologies, learn about new markets and new developments, acquire more knowledge and know-how, or learn a new language you think will be helpful to furtherer your business or professional growth, etc.

A human being is a social entity. So, social interactions and activities are most important. Give 25 per cent time to your family, relatives and friends. This will not only make you emotionally stronger, it will also provide you a cushion in the time of any business or personal setbacks.

What to do with the rest 25 per cent? It should go to your leisure activities, spending time in nature, unwinding, sports and exercises, hobbies such as photography, music, painting, cooking, gardening, writing, etc., whatever you want to do without any financial motive or string attached to it.

Such a balanced scheduling will make your life fulfilled and fill it with happiness and ever new enthusiasm. You will never have a dull or a wasted moment.

Enjoy your life and use your life gainfully, this is the basic philosophy of every successful person.

Come, live your life to the fullest by dividing it into perfect quarters.

29

Condo Projects: Your Best Bet in Realty

If you see the list of multi-millionaires and billionaires of the world, you'll find that many of them made their fortunes through real estate investing and development.

Global lists of billionaires are compiled every year by magazines such as *Forbes*, *Time* and some others. Among the top 100 of the richest, many are from the real estate business.

Tim Blixseth, Donald Trump, Akira Mori are the big names in real estate business world-wide. Equally, K. P. Singh, the DLF Group Chairman is one of the richest people in India.

Yes, my friend, real estate business has the highest potential of making one a multi-millionaire, and in quick time, too. Even in the coming years, this sector will be the most promising one in India to help you reach your goal faster.

In the coming years there would be tremendous demand for real estate and property world-wide, and particularly in India. And the reason is quite obvious.

Every year, thousands of educated young people graduate from colleges to enter the job market. They have big dreams about their careers and their personal lives. Within a few years, they start earning substantial salaries which fuel their quest for real estate. Buying a house is at the top of every successful young person's agenda. And there is no dearth of successful people in India. This is why property business in India is growing so rapidly.

Now, let us discuss a property related money-making idea which has the certain potential of creating a large number of multi-millionaires in the shortest possible time.

The idea is "condo projects".

Condo projects are very popular in the West but in India they are still few and far between. I envisage that in future there would be more and more condo projects in India and many Indians will become multi-millionaires based on such lucrative projects.

In the coming years families will be smaller, houses in the cities will be costlier, and most people will not be able to buy properties in the already developed urban areas. On the other hand, connectivity will improve. Roads, metros, trains will reach every corner of big city suburbs. People will buy more cars and would prefer living in the suburbs, free from congestion and pollution.

The result will be a proliferation of condo projects around the Indian metros. Here lies the exciting opportunity for aspiring multi-millionaires. Invest a million and get ready to earn multi-millions by planning and executing or marketing condos to an ever-growing clientele.

But what is a condo? It is the shorter form of the word, condominium. A condo is a form of property where a specified part of a piece of real estate — usually an apartment house — is individually owned while the use of, and access to, common facilities are controlled by the association of owners that represents the joint ownership of the whole piece.

Technically, a condominium is a collection of individual home units along with the land upon which they are built. Individual home ownership within a condominium is construed as ownership of only the space confining the boundaries of the home, i.e. the apartment. All common spaces have undivided ownership of a collective body established at the time of the condominium's creation. The body holds this property on behalf of the home owners as a group.

So, a condo has all the facilities without the exorbitant cost.

With joint families in India now dwindling, working couples busier than ever in their professions, domestic help becoming both demanding and scarce, the compact condo apartments are the need of the hour. Western lifestyle is becoming the norm among working couples in India as well, so condos are bound to be in great demand in the years to come.

People don't want to live in congested localities or suffocating city interiors burdened with traffic jams, pollution and escalating prices — they are moving out into the suburbs, surrounded by open spaces and in smart dwelling units. Also, many families now want a second home where they can spend their weekends or holidays, away the claustrophobic city experience. Which means that condos are here to stay.

The early birds are the winners, always. The condo idea is not yet widely perceived here in India, but it has huge potential. So, don't wait further. Start your own project before too many other people join the competition.

To keep yourself ahead of competition, find spaces in the metro suburbs at cheaper rates and start developing them. Chalk out what facilities you are going to provide there. Build club houses, develop playing areas, greens, swimming pool, departmental stores, medical facilities, religious places, play schools for children, crèches, tie up with movie hall and restaurant owners to set up their units, so on and so forth. Get the condo units connected with nice drivable roads connecting to the main roads. Get all the clearances and amenities, such as power, water and security arrangements from the local authorities.

You can also target India's tourist centres and major religious destinations as potential venues for condos. Once one of your projects becomes successful and financially profitable, target other Indian metros and big cities. Plan big condos, up to twenty floors. Think of spacious condos, where one entire floor is a single dwelling unit, etc.; there can be numerous variations to suit different customers.

As condos are still a novel concept in India, try to gather as much information about condos built in USA, in Canada, in Germany, in Japan and in Singapore. If possible, visit these countries and talk to their developers and builders to get a first hand account. If that's too expensive an option for you, go through various websites of international builders who are developing condos successfully.

I'm sure that if you concentrate on this unique idea and execute it diligently and industriously, nobody will be able to stop you from becoming a multi-millionaire, or even a billionaire within a few years.

Some years back I was on a cruise liner in Canada. The cruise ship was visiting numerous islands in and around Canada. I was surprised to see that islands with very sparse population, hardly twenty or twenty-five thousand each or less, had all the modern facilities — markets, hospitals, multiplexes and, of course, condos — for the island's population.

In one such place, I met the head of a construction company building condos. It was a sparsely populated place, but by Saturday evening I found the construction company people quite animated. All of their forty condos were sold out. Prices of the condos were on a higher side, but people were eager to move in and there was no looking back.

Why not repeat that kind of experience in India? At some twenty or thirty kilometres from the city or metro areas, both small and big type of condos can be built. Your profit is well assured.

If you don't have big money to build big condos, make the first a smaller one, pooling all your resources. You will be able to realize your big dreams, soon.

Nowadays, people are ready to pay more for comfort, luxury and prestige. So, even in smaller condos, provide all the latest amenities for a comfortable life, build a clubhouse for the residents. Those will be the hottest properties.

If the condo project is bigger, consisting of more than two hundred units, get a star hotel in the vicinity, a multiplex, a hospital and an office complex. Your project will attract more people and ultimately get booked in great numbers.

So, you see, becoming a multi-millionaire is not a big deal. Where there is a will, surely there is a way!

The concept of condo is one of such idea, which if properly implemented can do miracles. If you have any other such ideas, do write to me; my address is at the end of this book.

An idea is a seed. You should let it grow and blossom into a full fledged tree. This magic tree is your future money spinner.

30

Do Something — Differently

If you want to make it big in your business, want to earn more than others, you have to do something different.

Let me share with you a recent example. Earlier, whenever the government started building a new road, one main casualty used to be trees. To build new highways or widen existing roads, trees had to be cut in large numbers. The environmentalists started raising their voice against the practice and court interventions became a regular affair. The projects were either stopped midway or took much longer time to complete.

Then a company came up with a unique solution. Instead of cutting and killing the trees, they started transplanting them, i.e. shifting full-grown trees to new locations undamaged, with their roots and branches intact. For transplanting each tree, they were paid by the government an amount of ₹6,000. Now, that doesn't sound like such a big amount but if we consider the large number of trees that need transplanting, it adds up to a considerable sum.

Also, it serves two useful purposes. One, it saves grown trees from untimely death. Second, these ten-, fifteen- or twenty-year old trees are providing greenery in arid, tree-less areas, thus making them environmentally richer. There are only a few companies which have the expertise for such an intricate transplanting job. So the company I've mentioned here stands to make a big fortune.

What's exciting is that they are making money from something new, something quite different.

Do something new, unconventional and uncommon — your progress in business will also be exceptional.

In 1907, Dr. Maria Montessori started her first Montessori school in Rome, Italy, called "Casa dei Bambini" (Children's Home). That special school was the pioneer of the Montessori method of education which stresses on "spontaneous self-development". Today, even after a century it's still the most popular method of children's education, world-wide.

Around forty years back a young man named Karsanbhai Patel used to sell washing powder moving around Ahmedabad on his bicycle. Today, Nirma washing powder gives a run for their money to established MNCs and Karsanbhai's company has a turnover of thousands of crores and employs 15,000 people.

The Coca Cola Company was founded in 1886. The drink was sold initially as a patent medicine at soda fountains, which were popular in the United States at that time due to the belief that carbonated water was good for health. John Pemberton, the owner had claimed that Coca-Cola cured many diseases, including addiction, dyspepsia, neurasthenia and headache. Today, Coke is the most popular non-alcoholic beverage world-wide, and is sold in more than two hundred countries.

Then there is this hair cutting saloon in Delhi which serves sandwiches and coffee to its customers. Extending the same idea, Nirvana, a company which runs several such saloons, added cafeterias to its beauty parlours where you can get sandwiches, pizza, pasta, coffee, soup and mocktails. Going to saloons and waiting for your turn is now an enjoyable experience.

In USA, a company, calling america dot com, started a service that allows subscribers to call free within America.

So, a new business idea has tremendous potential. Only, you have to encash the novel idea to make a big fortune. Opportunities can strike anytime, anywhere.

Whatever applies to business in general, also applies to the medical profession. Recently, a team of doctors in the USA successfully transplanted a face. The forty-six year woman's face was seriously damaged. The non-stop full face transplant operation took twenty-two hours and a team of thirty doctors at Cleveland Clinic, under team leader Maria Siemionow, MD.

This operation not only changed the woman's life, it also inspired many others. There are so many people hiding from society because they are afraid to go to the grocery store, afraid to walk the streets because of a disfigured face.

And, when you do something different, money simply pours in from different directions!

Near the Arlanda Airport in Stockholm, Sweden, a person has begun a novel experience. He bought an old, abandoned Boeing 747 aircraft and transformed it into a "Jumbo Hostel"! In 2009, it was completely renovated and ready for occupants. It has twenty-five rooms, eighty-five beds and it occupies an area of 3,800 sq. ft. There are restaurants, nightclub and a special banquet for marriage ceremonies. For Swedish entrepreneur Oscar Dios, it was a novel experience and it clicked!

Like him, you could also try to do something new. Then you won't have to wait too long to be a multi-millionaire.

31

Five True Friends Are All You Need

Let me ask you how many friends you have. Most likely you will start counting and, after listing them on a piece of paper one by one, you'll answer that you have fifty friends or that you have a hundred friends, or even more.

True, but the list you've made contains people whom you know, those who you might meet in a party, in the bar, in a pub, on an outing or during a pleasure ride. We often consider all people we know as friends. To be successful, however, you also need a more select group of friends who will stand by you in times of your need, who will advise you in your hours of emergency, support you emotionally and even financially if the need arises. Those are your true friends. They may be very few in numbers but they can help you to overcome all your problems, share your burdens, and steer you in the direction of accomplishment.

Don't go by numbers. Having a large number of friends may demonstrate your popularity, but it doesn't reveal how many of them are your true friends. It is said that a friend in need is a friend, indeed. This old formula has stood the test of time.

So, if you want to be a multi-millionaire, select five of your most trustworthy friends. Friends with whom you can share your business strategies, from whom you can get most infallible business advice and suggestions, who will stand by you in times of your need and who will never hesitate to share your business and emotional problems alike.

And, from your side, you should also be prepared to reciprocate likewise. Whenever any one of them needs your assistance or advice, you should be there without the least hesitation, at any hour of the day or night.

Select from among the long list of your acquaintance, five long lasting, time tested, true friends. This selection will take you a long way in reaching your goal. Reciprocate the fair practices of friendship. Strengthen the bonds at all cost.

In a highly self-centred business world, your five true friends will provide you with the much needed emotional and intellectual companionship and camaraderie, making all your endeavours a success.

32

How Spirituality Helps You Succeed

There are no sure-fire mantras which can turn you into a multi-millionaire overnight. Hard work, a defined goal, and a keen focus on a success oriented strategy are what you need. Yet, there is no denying the fact that spirituality helps to a great extent in building your fortune.

When applied correctly and with firm devotion, spiritual mantras show remarkable results. The resonance of mantras creates a lot of beneficial effects, which turn the wheel of fortune in your favour. If you are expecting a big turnaround in your destiny, take out a little time from your busy schedule, sit quietly in meditation and start repeating your chosen mantra in a rhythmic manner. Your mind will grow quiet and free from commotion, your powers of concentration will sharpen and you'll feel more energetic and enthusiastic to conduct your business. As a result, your business will grow by leaps and bounds and bring you greater fame and fortune.

The chanting of mantras is a powerful mental exercise. Once you master it, things will start moving in your favour.

Though there is no stipulated time for chanting mantras, do it at a fixed time every day. It will then soon turn into a habit and your body clock will respond favourably. Sit in a quiet place, undisturbed by other activities, close your eyes and chant your special mantra for ten to fifteen minutes at a stretch. You will soon feel the resonance, the calmness, and awakening of confidence and energy within.

If you've an important business meet or an appointment with an important person — chant your mantra for a few minutes in seclusion before the appointment. You'll find yourself more confident and more concentrated — and your meeting will be a big success.

Before submitting a tender, you can apply this process to get better result.

Make it a habit to chant your favourite mantra in the morning and again for a few minutes before going to bed. This practice will yield highly beneficial results in all of your activities.

Which mantra should you chant? You can choose any mantra that you like best. Any mantra you chant with complete devotion and concentration will bring great results. If you can't think of a mantra yourself, I can suggest the chanting of "Om". You can elaborate on that by adding the name of your deity, like, "Om Namah Shivaya"! Chanting preferences can differ but when chanted in perfect rhythm and with pure devotion, they all show remarkable results.

The first stage of chanting a mantra is *Vachika Japa*. Here the mantra is chanted loudly. For first-timers, this kind of chanting is easier. It can be done even without closing your eyes. It creates an amazing reverberation in the surroundings as well as in your body. You feel a sense of well-being within and feel energized and empowered for bigger achievements.

Then comes the *Upanshu Japa*. Here the mantra is chanted by muttering it in a highly rhythmic manner. The lips keep on chanting without uttering the mantra in clear words. The eyes are kept half closed. After sometime, you can feel the difference it makes in your mind, in your body and in your surroundings. It empowers one from within.

The third type is *Manas Japa* (mental chanting), which is a superior way of chanting. It's soundless, the eyes are closed but the mind remains active.

The fourth type is *Likhit Japa* (written chanting). In this variation, the mantra is written and chanted continuously. This can be done between twenty to a hundred times per sitting. It is also known as *"Akshara Para Brahma Japa"*, through which one reaches the supreme stage of Mantra Japa and empowerment.

Whatever method of chanting you follow, it should be done with a pure mind and keen attentiveness. No disturbance of any kind, no stray thinking, no wandering of thoughts. Using the timeless mantra, "Om", creates a unique resonance in the mind which ripples into the body, creating a metamorphosis within you.

Your mind becomes more powerful, more concentrated and more focused. Your success becomes inevitable — because you are differently empowered now in your body and mind.

For an entrepreneur, regular Mantra Japa is a way of attaining excellence.

33

A Bigger Space for Your Business

Here is a suggestion if you want to see your business grow bigger.

Whenever you buy space for your factory, office or business outlet, take a bigger place than what you actually need. A bigger space may not seem necessary at that time but it will be a very prudent investment for your future. Tomorrow, when your business grows and suddenly you need more space, you may not be able to get any close by. Even if you do, you may have to fork out a larger sum for the same size of space.

When you are building your new factory, get a few acres more than your immediate requirement. You will protest that bigger space means more money locked up, and that you don't have that extra money. Fair enough, but make a bit more effort, approach the bank with that added budget for loan. Once you acquire a bigger space, it's ultimately going to give you a bigger return.

Tomorrow when your business grows and you start getting more orders to be delivered on time, you will need a bigger space to expand your production facility. Are you sure you'll get the adjacent plot at that time? Quite possibly, you won't! If you get it elsewhere, you will have to build it anew; you have to apply afresh for the whole set of government clearances and utilities, you have to appoint new workers in a new set-up, new technicians and managers. And, last of all, at that time the price of land would have escalated manifold. You will find that the additional cost may be too great and your business will then be constrained and suffer.

Keeping all these possibilities in mind, it's a very practical and prudent decision to go for a bigger space now.

Usually, buying a bigger space than the current requirement is no burden on an enthusiastic entrepreneur. Rather, it's an asset, a valuable asset for an aspiring multi-millionaire. First, it's bound to save you from a lot of additional investments in the future. Secondly, it's a ready solution for your monetary needs in the future.

If you are in no need or in no position to extend your factory or office in the coming years, you can sell off that extra space. The return will be much more than your original investment. You can then re-invest this additional amount of money to extend your business. This is the way a successful businessman thinks. This is the way one grows to be a multi-millionaire.

Rent for spaces climbs higher every year but the availability of land and space in a particular area remains uncertain, so it's always a practical decision to get some additional space for your business or office right from the very beginning. This will be highly beneficial in the long run. You don't later have to hire extra space at an exorbitant price when any future requirement arises. Also, you will be able to expand your operations easily without any extra burden on you.

In particular, if you are buying land from government allotment for constructing your office or factory, get a bigger space at any cost. This will put you into an advantageous position with readily available surplus land to extend your factory. And in case you sell it after some years, you will earn much more than what you can imagine. A little forethought will bring you a lot of benefits!

34

Say No to Over-Trading

Many people start over-trading in the hope of building a bigger business and a bigger fortune overnight!

No doubt one can over-trade somewhat in good times but if this habit becomes a part and parcel of your business, it can result in serious consequences.

If you get addicted to over-trading, it creates havoc by placing you in a vulnerable position. In times of tough business conditions, you can get badly trapped, unable to get out of the vicious circle. It ultimately stops one's business growth altogether, and the various avenues of progress start closing one after the other, a big uncertainty looms ahead, losses pile up and the business falls flat on its face.

For example, a builder who uses the advance money received from prospective buyers of a particular project for buying plots for new projects gets into over-trading without knowing the consequences. He becomes entangled in a lot of projects without adequate financial backing, and each of the projects suffers in consequence. The advance money he had received for his initial project never bears fruit. The project either remains unfinished, or never even starts.

Naturally, the customers feel cheated. They seek their money back or take legal recourse for its recovery. The builder thus gets entangled in a vicious circle and, gradually, all his projects either get delayed or are abandoned. Heavy penalties, litigation, bad press, pressure from the banks and customers asking for their money back — all these become his daily routine. His reputation suffers, his credibility falls drastically and ultimately he finds himself stuck at a dead end.

There are so many miserable cases related to over-trading practice by overzealous businessmen. No one ever benefits from habitual over-trading. It's the most reckless and disastrous way of doing business. Beware, never fall into this trap.

Most recently, a known property developer bought a huge bungalow with the advance money he had received for a forthcoming project of his. He thought he would be able to make a fast buck by selling the luxurious bungalow within a few months at a handsome profit. He could then continue his planned project in a big way.

But something unexpected awaited him. An economic meltdown sealed his fate. Property prices came down heavily. There was no buyer in the market for the bungalow. He got trapped. The money he'd collected as advance payments from customers got stuck, no new customer was available in the market and his project got stalled.

Over-trading is a vicious circle. It ends many dreams and many promising futures. If you ever get caught in its grip, get back to your normal course in quick time, before it's too late.

Don't play tricks with your customers, deliver what you've promised in time; never hide anything from your prospective clientele and be true to your commitment.

Honesty never lets one down. In fact, an honest businessman earns both a high reputation as well as riches in the course of time.

35

Give Some Rest to Your Mind

Any businessman, especially an aspiring multi-millionaire is a busy person. Then, too, almost every businessman has this tendency to mull over his business activities and happenings day and night, even when it's time to go to bed! Such over-thinking is somehow like an obsession which you should be very wary of.

You need to practise the art of giving rest to your mind. If you are mentally worried, not sleeping well and always overburdened with multiple and obsessive thoughts, it will prove counter-productive. A relaxed mind helps you to concentrate, to solve problems and plan future strategies.

Thinking about your business should undoubtedly be a part of your daily routine. It's normal and spontaneous. But when it turns into constant worry and obsession, it's not going to help you in any way. Rather, it will take its toll and harm your health. High blood pressure, irritation, digestive disorder, lack of concentration, forgetfulness, even heart problems — these are the ultimate result of excessive thinking and lack of mental rest.

Obviously, you don't want your business to be affected by chronic mental disturbances. So, it's urgent to learn the art of giving rest to your mind amidst a highly active life. Make your mind calm, cool and composed. Put a full stop to all your stray thoughts, or at least to the overflow of random, superfluous thoughts.

When your mind is uncluttered and relaxed, its power and intensity grows, as also its ability to focus and co-ordinate. A successful businessman will always take care of this very crucial aspect related to his business growth. A peaceful mind ensures prosperity.

But how to put a brake on unbridled thoughts?

It seems impossible to put a brake on one's thoughts. People think that the mind works spontaneously and continuously, without any human interference. What role does one play consciously in the thought process? The fact is that putting a brake on random thoughts is very much possible and that it is well within our reach.

Follow this simple exercise. Lie down and relax your whole body. Try to put a full stop to your thoughts. Become just a spectator of everything around you, don't react or interact. Just keep on watching, putting your mind at rest.

Once you close your eyes, try to visualise each and every limb of your body through your mind's eyes. Perceive your right leg and toes. Then shift to your left leg and toes, then your right hand, right palm, and the fingers followed by the left hand, left palm and the fingers. Try to imagine your face with your eyes closed. It's a different kind of experience. Try to feel, without touching, how tired your facial skin has become due to tension and mental strife. Feel your body totally relax, your mind unburden, and your tension is gone! Lying with your eyes closed, continue your inward journey to your eyes, nose, lips, mouth, ears and, ultimately, to your mind.

Keep your eyes closed, your mind calm and quiet and your body motionless. Your mental journey will continue to travel to every part of your body smoothly and effortlessly. You'll start feeling a change, a never before experienced change in your mind and your body. Peace and tranquillity will prevail, bestowing you with extraordinary mental power, energy and enthusiasm.

You will feel relaxed, fortified with new energy and absolutely tension-free. You will be a changed person now, with more eagerness to execute your job, and think more purposefully.

Take out just fifteen minutes every day from your busy schedule and invest that precious time in creating a healthy and harmonious environment in your mind. You will definitely mark a metamorphosis within yourself. You will gradually experience a completely relaxed mind and an agile body. Your business will start growing, so will your confidence. Depression, restlessness and fatigue will be things of the past!

Whenever you feel overwhelmed by endless thoughts, or burdened by the pressure of confused thinking, apply this art of stopping your thoughts and unburdening your mind. Once you make it a regular practice, you will feel a remarkable improvement in all your activities, in your life and in your business fortunes.

36

Spend Just Two Per Cent in Charity and See Miracles Happen

If I use the term PC, you will obviously think that I'm talking of a personal computer. But, no, I am not talking about computers. The PC I'm referring to is something which can contribute in taking your business a big step forward towards prosperity. And there is no looking back either. The two per cent PC formula is a powerful catalyst of assured business growth.

What is this formula we are talking about? It's a promise you make that you will always spend two per cent of your income in PC, which ultimately ensures a steady progress for your business. And here PC stands for personal charity.

Personal charity is an aspect of a progressive business approach. It's also the social responsibility of a prosperous businessman, a due he pays to the society in acknowledgement of the role the society plays in nurturing a person and his dreams.

Two per cent of your business income for personal charity is not a very big amount to spend — and it pays back in a big way in the growth of your business.

You can't believe how effective this formula of 2 per cent PC is. I've seen its efficacy many a time in my long career as a business consultant. This is a miracle waiting to happen. All over India, entrepreneurs who have unhesitatingly adopted this policy have flourished manifold.

How does it happen? Firstly, it gives you immense satisfaction and this makes you happier and more enthusiastic to work harder and earn more. Secondly, there is this spiritual influence, which turns the wheel of fortune in your favour. The good wishes of the people, the blessings of the Supreme Being, and lastly the benediction from the hearts of hundreds of deprived people of society — all these create good vibes around you and your business, resulting in excellence.

Through 2 per cent PC you help the most deprived people in the society, people who have no one to reach out to for help. This is not just money, it's an honest motivation beyond just money making, a call of urgency from the core of your heart.

There are so many people who remain hungry most of the time. People sleep on the pavements in chilly winter nights. People have no money to buy medicines for themselves or their children. For many people, education remains a distant dream. If you try to help these people according to your capacity — you get a never before experienced satisfaction, zeal to do something better for the people and the society around us.

Your mind becomes contented, elated and engaged in doing the best. And this satisfaction is a great thing which motivates people to achieve the extraordinary. This ultimately lifts you up, your spirit, your prospects to the level of the extraordinary.

I get letters from business people from all over India. They vouch for this unique formula of two per cent PC and tell me that the result is most impressive. The miraculous result of PC starts showing right away.

If so many people are applying it as a part of business and a number of people are pretty sure about the outcome — there is no reason why you shouldn't also assume this practice. Apply it today as an integral part of your business and let amazing things happen in your business, too.

Make sure of one thing, though; never undertake it for self gratification, pride or publicity. Make it a very private affair, free from boasting and self promotion. Don't ever make it into a PR exercise or a media event. The main cause will then be defeated.

Whether you are a small or a big entrepreneur, it makes no difference. The policy is the same. Make it a part of your core business policy that you will spend two per cent of your business profits in personal charity. Within six months you will see the difference — your business will definitely prosper.

Tell your friends and colleagues as well about this two per cent PC formula. And write to me and tell me the results of your experience with two per cent PC.

Recently, I met a young IT professional who works in a big company. He voluntarily spends some of his free time teaching English to children living in the slums and he really enjoys doing so. As a top corporate executive, he earns a big salary and drives a big car. But the satisfaction he derives from his voluntary teaching is something special. The other day he arranged a few more big cars from his friends and took all the kids he teaches for a joy ride, then to a movie, and later on to a hotel for a grand treat. He explained to the children about the necessity of education and hard work for a better future. He instilled hope in their hearts that anyone can reach the pinnacle of success through education, regular study habits, a positive attitude and hard work.

Such activities give one immense pleasure and peace of mind — and that's a big reward in itself. And by pursuing the formula of two per cent PC you are bestowed with many more rewards — which ultimately propel your business to prosperity.

37

Steer Clear of Credit Card Debt

Plastic money is in vogue these days. Anyone and everyone goes around flashing two, three or four credit cards to show that he or she has "arrived".

Instant purchases are made easier due to credit cards. It's called impulsive buying. You see something in a shop window and you can buy it immediately even if you are not carrying any money. You simply fish out a credit card from your wallet and hand it over to the shop attendant. It's that simple!

There is little doubt that credit cards are a great convenience. You don't have to carry unnecessarily large amounts of cash as safeguard against any unexpectedly heavy expense that may arise.

The convenience of a credit card as a cash-substitute is one thing. But using it to run up debt on a continuous basis is quite another. You can get into this trap without your even realizing it but the repercussion is a hazard to your financial health. My earnest suggestion is, steer clear of credit card debt at any cost.

If you want to run a profitable business, your first and foremost duty is to be in control of your expenses and keeping a tab on all expenditure. Credit card users always overstep the limit and get entangled in unnecessary dues which grow by leaps and bounds. So, the use of credit cards should be kept to the absolute minimum by an aspiring multi-millionaire. When you use your credit for convenience of payment, rather than to get into debt, make sure you pay back the entire dues in one go and well in time.

If you don't pay the due amount in time, you pay hefty interest on it. You should be aware that credit cards charge an exorbitant amount on interest on overdues, eating into your income. This is not a healthy trend for a promising businessman. So, it's better to avoid using credit cards for business debts.

Not only that; also instruct your wife and children not to run up continuous debts on their credit cards.

Give strict instruction to your accounts department to pay your credit card bills immediately. If any credit card bill does not arrive in time, call up the credit card issuing company or send them an e-mail asking for the bills. If your payments are not made within the billing cycle, you are left with no option but to pay hefty interest, in addition to the due amount. There are penalties for late payments as well.

Also, people often end up buying many unnecessary things *via* credit cards. You get tempted to visit expensive eateries or buy overpriced clothes and fashion accessories — because you don't need to pay in cash at the time of purchase; just a swipe of the credit card is all that is required! You must learn to steer clear of such temptations.

So, if you are really serious about earning a big fortune, be cautious about running up credit card debts.

38

Not By Degrees Alone

Education is useful for career growth. But it's not essential. A coveted degree is not the prerequisite for becoming a multi-millionaire. What is important is to work hard at what you are inclined to and find interest in and that is what will boost your success and financial growth.

There are thousands of highly successful entrepreneurs in the world who were big flops in their college education. G. D. Birla was one such entrepreneur who, despite his lack of educational qualification and university degrees, concentrated on building his vast business empire and became one of India's richest businessmen.

So, lack of educational qualification is no handicap for an aspiring multi-millionaire. People who are planning to become big entrepreneurs should concentrate more on their business, rather than on acquiring all sorts of educational qualifications.

Walt Disney is recognized world-wide for his impact on the field of entertainment. He became one of the best-known motion picture producers in the world and the creator of the fabled Disneyland. He never studied beyond school. Disney dropped out of high school at the age of sixteen to join the Army, but the Army rejected him. He considered becoming a newspaper artist, drawing political comic strips. He visited numerous newspaper offices but nobody wanted to hire him as an artist, or even as a driver. But he made it big through his tenacity and sheer confidence.

When asked about it he said, "If you have a dream, you can realise it, too." This is the basic mantra for success in one's life.

If you lack higher educational qualification and think that this will hamper your progress, think again — there are many successful entrepreneurs in the world who have never crossed the threshold of a college or dropped out of one!

The CEO of Apple Computers, Steve Jobs, is one such icon. In 1972, Jobs enrolled in Reed College in Portland, Oregon but dropped out after one semester.

While addressing students at Stanford University on 12 January 2005, Jobs told them that he dropped out of college within six months of enrolment. He felt that he was wasting the hard earned money and savings of his parents by enrolling in an expensive course. What he was seeking in life was not just pursuing a college degree, but something else — so he thought it would be better if he did something by himself.

According to him, ". . . I naively chose a college that was almost as expensive as Stanford, and all of my working-class parents' savings were being spent on my college tuition. After six months, I couldn't see the value in it. I had no idea what I wanted to do with my life and no idea how college was going to help me figure it out. And here I was spending all of the money my parents had saved their entire life. So I decided to drop out and trust that it would all work out OK. It was pretty scary at the time, but looking back it was one of the best decisions I ever made . . . ."

He had no place to sleep in those days. He shared rooms with his friends, mostly sleeping on the floor. For food, he would often walk several kilometres to eat free meals supplied at the ISCKON temple.

Later, when he became successful in life, he used to remember those days of despair. But he never lost either his enthusiasm or his direction and diligently followed his dreams.

Jobs advises the young never to lose hope in any situation. Tenacity ultimately triumphs. And that's the core belief behind every phenomenal success.

According to Steve Jobs, people should not be obsessed with problems and limitations. Nothing can stop a determined person from achieving his goal. Later in life, Jobs was diagnosed with cancer of the pancreas and the doctors were not very hopeful about being able to cure it. But Jobs was not scared at all. His will-power and positive attitude led to a miracle; he was cured after an operation but without chemotherapy! Not once but twice he was diagnosed with serious ailments and he had to take leave from his job. His deputies were assigned as acting CEOs for months at a time. But he came back every time after getting cured, with new ideas and new projects.

His phenomenal life teaches us one thing. Keep on doing what you love to do. Don't be distracted, don't be disheartened. Time is short and you have to do a lot of things in your life. There is no time for pessimistic thoughts. Always be guided by your inner instincts.

And, according to Jobs, the core mantra of his outstanding success can be summarized by the phrase: "Stay hungry, stay foolish".

Or, take the case of Bill Gates. Bill Gates also did not complete a college degree. But information technology (IT) was always his favourite and at the core of his activities. Ultimately, he succeeded in his chosen realm. Path-breaking new ideas and their implementation, with keen pursuance — these are the key ingredients that made Bill Gates a phenomenal success.

N. R. Narayana Murthy, the founder of Infosys always insists on a few key points: Never be dependent on one technology, one idea, one client, one person, even on one country, to make it big in the business arena. If you want to make rapid progress in life and in business, bring fresh new air into it.

J. K. Rowling, the creator of the Harry Potter series of best-selling books, is another truly inspiring personality. Rowling is known for her rags-to-riches life, in which she progressed from living on social welfare to a billionaire status within just five years.

Ever since she was a child she had this dream to be a writer. But for long she had to be satisfied with jobs like that of a secretary or translator. Her mother died after a ten-year struggle with multiple sclerosis and with a broken heart that her daughter was quite unsuccessful in life, financially or otherwise. Rowling moved to Portugal to teach English, married but divorced after a year. She now had a daughter to support as a single mother.

During this period, Rowling was diagnosed with clinical depression, and even contemplated suicide.

But at the same time she was busy with the idea of Harry Potter and was writing her first book. A small-time London publisher advised her that young readers might not like to read something written by a female author. So she had to use as her pen name, the "masculine sounding" J. K. Rowling, instead of Joanne Rowling. She wrote the entire book on an old manual typewriter, sitting in inexpensive cafes day after day, over cups of black coffee and sandwiches.

It saved her from the heating costs during the chilly English winter months and her two year old daughter was able to sleep comfortably in the warm cafés.

A single mother with no regular source of income, no one to fall back upon and supported by meagre state welfare money, had only her big ideas and an old typewriter to depend on. And how she succeeded in proving her mettle! Today, her net worth is in billions.

In June 2008, while talking to the students of Harvard University, Rowling said that it was not poverty that disturbed her in those pre-Harry Potter days, but it was the lack of success that tormented her through all those years.

According to her, success in life is not about chronicling a series of successful accomplishments or the making of a highly outstanding bio-data; it's about winning against all odds, overcoming all failures.

Thus, the power we need for our success is in our thoughts. We have that vast resource of hidden power within us, which can withstand and win against all adversities in life

Warren Buffett, the Chairman and CEO of the US company Berkshire Hathaway, is among the richest people in the world. He is known as the "Legendary Investor". This eighty-plus business tycoon simply depends on his intellect and outstanding thinking ability to earn his billions, and even in this era of IT revolution seldom uses the marvels of IT.

Once he remarked, "If Calculus or Algebra were required to be a great investor, I'd have to go back to delivering newspapers."

According to him, "Stock market investment should follow the techniques of an ace baseball player. You get to stand at the place all day, and you never have to hit if you don't want to. You get to see every pitch. You learn the pitcher, his moves, his technique, his faults, and then only when you want to, if you want to at all, you get to swing the bat. Only in the stock market can you use this technique. You can wait a year or two for the perfect situation to come along, and only then, you play, or you can trade every day as a momentum investor, and see where you wind up."

As he summed up, "The stock market is a no-called-strike game. You don't have to swing at everything — you can wait for your pitch."

According to Buffett, the most crucial investment one can make is on one's own life. It's the most precious thing and should be managed for optimum results. It's like a car you've to drive for your entire life. You should keep it at the top of its capacity, functionally perfect and well maintained.

Buffet's advice to entrepreneurs is never to think about retirement: "You are as agile and active as your mental ability. Never think of yourself as an old person, your mind never retires."

Robert Kiyosaki, the American business investor is better known for his world famous series of *Rich Dad Poor Dad* books. According to him, formal education is only for the job seekers; for businessmen, success depends on experience, insights and ability.

He stressed on three things for success in business: cash flow management, time management to create a perfect balance between professional and personal life and, thirdly, people management.

Nowadays, most young families comprise of two earning members. Typically, both husband and wife are working professionals and contribute to the family kitty. I would say that there should be three earning members in the family, not two, namely you, your spouse and, thirdly, your money. The money you and your wife have saved should be invested in such a way that it starts earning profits for your family. This means prudent and productive investment. You should start thinking in this new way of creating surplus income every month. This will also take care of your post-retirement financial blues. Even in business, you should start investing your surplus money in the most productive way. Cash flow should always be on the rise for a successful business outcome.

Well, I've advocated all along that college or university degrees are not necessary for business excellence. That's true. But that does not mean that one should not keep oneself aloof from acquiring knowledge, especially knowledge that serves one's business purpose. If you are a successful businessman, you should definitely know how to read a balance sheet, not the way a professional accountant might interpret it, but you should be able to comprehend it. Also, you should have essential knowledge of corporate law and other legal matters that impact your business. No doubt, your managers and accountants or company secretary are the competent people to deal with these matters on a day-to-day basis, but it's not an ideal situation if you are completely uninformed about these various facets of business.

And, lastly, you should also learn to save money in your business and use that saved amount to make prudent investments leading to growth.

39

Do Something New in Realty

It's hardly surprising that the realty business goes through ups and downs. All businesses are affected by the business cycle. For an enthusiastic entrepreneur who wants to become a multi-millionaire, a dull phase is the most opportune moment of making a move in realty. If you are astute, such times offer those rare yet most exciting opportunities for making fabulous profits.

For example, in the 2008 economic downturn a builder came up with a novel way of making profits despite a sluggish market and reluctant customers. It's a well known fact that in a financially tight market, liquidity is the biggest problem. So, what should a builder do? This particular one applied his presence of mind and decided to use the barter system. And, lo, in a lifeless period of real estate business, he made some exciting profits.

He put out a nicely created advertisement in the newspapers and invited building material suppliers to provide him with building materials in lieu of free space in his ongoing and forthcoming real estate projects. This was a kind of partnership which was novel, indeed — and very profitable, too.

Suppliers of steel and iron, cement, electrical equipment suppliers and sanitary ware suppliers, all found the offer lucrative. They all were eager to clinch deals. In lieu, they acquired premium space for their shops and offices within the builder's various projects, guaranteed space in his forthcoming malls and even flats and vacant plots — it turned out to be a most profitable barter deal for all concerned.

It was not just the builder who benefited from the deal. Everyone did. In a time of recession, building material suppliers were also hit by a lack of business. So, when this unique barter offer arrived on a platter, they were more than happy at the prospect of getting space in shopping malls or acquiring land in tomorrow's townships with no cash investment, and that too at very favourable rates. It was a highly profitable deal indeed.

The moral of the story is that never be disheartened in any situation. Don't consider yourself helpless or luckless. Every situation has two sides to it. Always look at the positive side of everything. Those who are aspiring to be multi-millionaires should make note of it. Even severe recession can be turned into profitable propositions.

The real estate business in India is flourishing, especially in the mid-range and smaller cities. All the recent surveys on Indian real estate trends suggest that non-metro cities have more potential and possibilities. Things are really happening there. So, an entrepreneur who wants to be a multi-millionaire faster, should keep an eye on this growing trend.

An estimate about the bank loans in Indian cities has revealed some startling facts. In Gangtok, the capital of Sikkim, for example, one in every four people has taken a home loan! In Bhubaneshwar, the capital of Orissa, one out of five people has acquired a home loan to purchase his home. This highlights the bright prospects for a real estate investor. Smaller cities, smaller homes, but the possibility and potential are big enough to make an aspiring multi-millionaire take note of this vast realm, full of opportunities.

Another niche area where there is a big opportunity is buying and selling of islands. In the West, big businessmen, film stars and developers buy islands in far-off areas, like in the South Pacific or in the Mediterranean. In Canada and in the USA, there are smaller islands on the rivers too. In India people are not much aware of such a trend. But, sometime back I read a news item that a small island off the Kerala coast was sold for a few crores! If you get such an opportunity, buy it after ascertaining its ownership. Selling it to a rich businessman or a film star after a few years can net you huge profit.

What I'm trying to say is that you should try and do something new, something different from the others, and this will bring the maximum profit into your kitty. The real estate business has huge potential for new, exciting ideas. Come up with new ideas and unique, well planned business strategies. Success lies well within your abilities.

Shopping malls are today's business reality in India. Whether it's Ambala or Ahmedabad, Gurgaon or Guwahati — malls are everywhere! In fact, in some cities there are more malls than are required. Take the example of Faridabad. On the stretch of Mathura Road running between Delhi and Faridabad, there are already so many existing shopping malls and newer ones are still constantly coming up.

Of course, not every mall will be a big success. Many of them will flop or close down within a few years if they are not planned properly. Also, you can't build so many malls in such close proximity to one another; departmental Stores and malls differ. Why would a prospective buyer visit a particular shopping mall? Price difference can't be great in today's highly competitive market.

So if you're in the real estate business and planning to build shopping malls, plan well. Avoid building smaller malls which have limited amenities. These will not turn a profit for a long time.

A bigger shopping mall with multiplexes, a large number of eateries, a spa, beauty saloons, gift shops, latest fashion outlets, banks, ATMs, pubs and coffee shops, lots of open space, a huge parking lot, children's play area, greenery and attractive landscaping, even a couple of boutique or star hotels within the mall are what will attract more business for you and assure bigger footfalls for the business owners in your mall.

Visit some of those stunning shopping malls in Singapore, Hong Kong, Malaysia, Dubai and elsewhere and try to chalk out your future plans based on what you learn from them and reap the richness of profit in real estate business.

Small families, smaller investments, small flats — this trend is now in vogue. Many property developers are now stressing on affordable properties for middle class families. If you can provide them with plenty of amenities, such as a club, a community centre, mini shopping mall, nursing home, play grounds and green areas without taxing their limited budgets, your housing projects will be a big hit and turn out to be big profit making ventures.

There is another business practice which is often employed in Europe and America but which is not yet in vogue in India. This is an idea especially for those who have limited resources but big dreams.

Buy a dilapidated property and renovate it. Put in all modern amenities, re-do, repair and refurbish the structure and make it a highly attractive property. Then sell it and make big profit. Many property seekers seek independent properties in good locations, but they don't have much time for building or repairing them.

They are your prospective buyers. Once you specialize in such properties and earn a name in the market, no one can stop you from becoming a multi-millionaire.

If you are thinking of entering the real estate business, don't hesitate any more. It's one of the best profit making business sectors. If you don't have any experience in the trade, it doesn't matter. You will pick up the nuances of this industry as you go along. And if you don't have many resources to start with, again don't be disheartened. Property business is one area where you can become a multi-millionaire in the fastest possible time.

40

Final Thoughts

We are now nearing the end of this book. Our prime concern is how to become a multi-millionaire, surpassing the status of an average businessman.

The very first thing you should do to reach your goal is to take a vow that you will never give up on your dream. Try to repeat this thought in your mind: "There are hundreds of multi-millionaires today, why can't I be one!"

Our scriptures, our tradition have always taught us: "You get what you expect!"

Just be determined and work hard to achieve your goal. Be confident about the outcome and, soon, you will be a winner. If you have a rock solid will and dogged ability to pursue your dream, nothing can stop you from becoming a multi-millionaire.

Read the biographies of those who have reached the pinnacle of success starting from an ordinary level. Visit the local public library and discover the huge number of successful real life achievers and entrepreneurs who are truly self made and who started just from scratch.

Magazines, websites — everywhere you will come across inspirational ideas, episodes and anecdotes related to money-making miracles. These sources will inspire you to follow in their footsteps and achieve phenomenal success.

If you want to become a multi-millionaire, develop your mindset accordingly. You will then be bubbling with energy and enthusiasm all the time. No negative thoughts, no departure from your path of action. You should always keep on moving ahead, adding to your experience with ever new ideas, innovations and technology.

Saving money should be your top priority. Useless and unnecessary expenditure should be curtailed. A successful businessman is always a prudent spender; he knows that money saved in the course of business is money earned.

No show off, no pomp, no unnecessary expenditure, this should be your policy. Don't throw big parties or move in big luxurious cars until you have become a multi-millionaire. You are at the threshold of some big achievement, work for it diligently. Parties can easily wait till then.

Save every paisa now and invest your hard-earned money back into your business. This is the time for self control. It's the time for honesty and real hard work.

Sometimes you hear of people who have made a lot of money through unfair means, tax theft or other dubious practices. Don't give much importance to such hearsay. Such people often get embroiled in monetary scandals or controversies and suffer business setbacks. There is no short cut to success, neither an unfair way to it. So many large business establishments, banks, multinationals have fallen flat on their face in recent years as a result of dishonest conduct. Honesty is the one and only policy that sustains a business endeavour and its success.

Take out ten to fifteen minutes everyday for thinking of your business goals and plans. Practice meditation. Your concentration and will-power will increase. Your body and mind will become fit as a fiddle, propelling all your thoughts and activities to the path of progress.

If you are new in business, there is no need to be embarrassed about your lack of knowledge or experience. Everyone starts from the beginning and matures over time.

There are so many ace businessmen who have shown exemplary progress over the years. Try to emulate some such person. Meet him and try to learn the secrets of success from him. Make him a role model, make him your business guru, in order to learn more about business growth.

Take care of the needs and welfare of your office staff. They are the backbone of your business. Pay them properly and in time. Encourage them. To make them sincere and punctual, reach your office well ahead of others and leave after everyone else. This will bring about a feeling of responsibility and the spirit of camaraderie among them.

Keep a watch on your competitors, their work and activities, their progress and business additions from time to time. Only then will you be able to make better and faster progress.

Tension and worries are also an integral part of life. When you have attained success, sometimes you will find yourself in a lonely or dejected state of mind. Uncertainties, complications and lack of inspiration may overwhelm your mind. You then feel helpless and unenthusiastic about everything. These are temporary phases that everyone encounters in a busy, tension ridden life. Don't overemphasize it. It will pass away soon.

Keep yourself busy with your work and be in the right state of mind. Work with a very holistic mindset. Think of yourself as a part of God's bigger plans. Follow the basic tenets of *Bhagavad-Gita*, do everything selflessly. Consider everything as your divine duty to fulfil higher goals. It will ease up your tensions and free you from loneliness and ennui. You will then find greater interest in your work and fewer detours on the way to your progress.

If you want to go abroad to earn big fortune, there are many avenues open these days. But in today's circumstances India offers the biggest opportunities for industrious and optimistic people. You can make a big fortune here, being among your own people, within a known social, political, economic and legal system. Every year, thousands of previously unknown people become multi-millionaires in India. They achieve tremendous success by the dint of their insight, innovations, inspiration and sheer hard work. Just think about it and question yourself, if they can be successful in their respective efforts, why shouldn't I! All your hesitations and reservations will melt away, leading you to a higher level of success.

Think about the society we live in. As we have duties towards our families, we have duties towards our society, too.

Once you are a multi-millionaire, gone are the days when you were lacking money and everything in your life was strictly budgeted. Now you have money to spare. Spend a part of that money for the welfare of society.

Think about those young people who are less fortunate, those who are looking for better opportunities to make their lives productive and fulfilling. Try to assist them and help them to progress and fulfil their dreams. They will look at you as their mentor and ideal. Helping others to prosper will be a matter of big satisfaction for you. This will be your way of paying back to the society, in acknowledgement of the role society has played in your progress and prosperity. In today's language, we will call it corporate social responsibility.

Some small things have a big significance in business and in the life of a successful businessman. Always try to appoint able and efficient people in your business. Such people will help you in nurturing and growing your business. You may have outstanding personal ability and great acumen in business tactics, but you need other people to take your business and profits to a greater height.

Customers are supreme in every business. Always be attentive to your customers and their problems. Try to give attention to each and every customer complaint. This is absolutely vital for the goodwill and sustainability of any business entity. A bad reputation will not only mar your prospects, it will drive away your prospective customers. If even after repeated attempts, your staff is unable to satisfy a customer, try to handle it personally. If possible, meet the client for feedback. Ask for his suggestions, and his ideas. In this way, each case will be a valuable lesson for you, which will ultimately help in your progress.

Save, save and save! This should be the motto of every successful businessman. Benjamin Franklin, the noted scientist, inventor and statesman once said, "If you can run your family well and save money, consider yourself fortunate enough. As if, you have the possession of 'touchstone' which can turn every occasion into a golden opportunity!"

Save money and invest it back into your business. This is one of the biggest secrets of continuous business growth.

Whenever you are initiating something in your business, or starting a new business, think carefully of all the pros and cons and weigh every related problem and prospect. Don't do anything without proper thinking and deliberation; don't do anything in a hurry. Take your time, be patient and take responsibility for all your actions.

There is this old saying:

"I'm in a hurry to get things done.
Oh, I rush and rush until life's no fun.
All I really gotta do is live
and die
But I'm in a hurry and don't know why."

Rash decision or rash driving, neither helps; in fact, both prove risky.

Each and every action of yours should be helpful and beneficial for your business. But we should do nothing which would hurt others' interests or we will have to repent later.

Business is directed by self-interest, but it should not be equated with selfishness. The philosophy of "selfless duty" (*Nishkam Karma* according to the *Bhagavad Gita*) should be your preferred course of action. Only then would you be able to get rid of unnecessary tension and mental stress. "I'm just doing my duty ordained to me. I will perform it without unnecessary attachment to its outcome. The end result depends on the Supreme Being, not me!" This unique attitude will save you from all untoward outcomes and give you peace of mind. As a result, your business will take the course of natural abundance and prosperity.

While addressing an audience in Toronto, Canada, Swami Dayananda said:

> "Remember a single working day of ten or twelve hours when you were free from expectations! In sleeping hours at night we are free from wishes and expectations, but in the wakeful hours, why are we are to control our thoughts!"

Chanakya Sutra, the ancient Indian treatise says:

Yo yasmin karmani kushalah sa tasmin yoktavyah.

The meaning is: Whoever is an expert in whichever field, should be engaged in that.

This should be the cardinal practice of a successful entrepreneur. To become successful, you should be engaged in a job in which you have keen interest, inclination and ability. Always make a choice according to your interest and aptitude, not just based on what someone may have suggested to you or by trying to mindlessly ape what others are doing successfully.

Success comes from a pursuit which makes you happy and satisfied. And that's the pre-requisite of prosperity.

Chanakya Sutra is full of practical advice which can contribute substantially to your success. For example, it says that if any worker in your office misappropriates office money, he should be punished, but if a loss occurs for which no office staff is responsible, they should not be blamed or put under pressure. Everyone should be rewarded for his achievement and adherence to duty. These are the various ingredients which add up to eventual success.

A successful businessman never allows unfounded thoughts and phobias to govern his activities. He thinks positively and in moments of crises, he remains unperturbed and unruffled. He knows that every situation is a learning stage and every crisis will pass, bringing new opportunities and hope.

A successful person always thinks in a constructive way and knows that, God willing, nothing can stop him from attaining success once he is on the right track.

Obstacles and adversities are a part of life, one should not lose one's cool in such situations. Every able and experienced businessman knows that every problem is transitory and can be dealt by adopting the right strategy. Persistence can overcome all adversities.

> "Nothing in this world can take the place of persistence. Talent will not, nothing is more common than unsuccessful people with talent. Genius will not; unrewarded genius is almost a proverb. Education will not; the world is full of educated derelicts. Persistence and determination alone are omnipotent. The slogan 'press on' has solved and always will solve the problems of the human race."
>
> — Calvin Coolidge

Brihadaranyaka Upanishad says: "You are what your deep driving desire is."

Know what your strengths and weaknesses are. I still remember what the world renowned yoga teacher B.K.S. Iyengar had once said during a discussion with his disciples, "At an early age of seventeen I came to know about my weakness about formal education. That's why I've never attended any college. Still I'm teaching college students!"

At the age of ninety, when he was still actively teaching yoga, he said that he was still a student of yoga even at that age.

One should never stop learning. You must cultivate this as a lifelong process. Once a person stops learning, he becomes inert and uninterested, which hampers the process of continuous growth.

One should keep oneself updated about what is happening in the world of business and industry. It will keep one progressive in one's attitude and activities, add advantage to one's business moves which will ultimately ensure one's business growth.

One can learn about the latest trends and technologies in the field of one's particular industry by studying various journals and trade magazines. Either one can subscribe to them or become a member of a good library. The USIS Library in Indian metros is a rich source of such publications. Also, using the Internet for relevant information is now often the best alternative. Take some time out of your busy schedule to surf the Internet and read magazines; this will help you in increasing your wealth in the long run.

It is possible to achieve whatever you wish to once you have the right idea backed by strong will-power and readiness to work hard. And the power you need for your success is within you. Concentrate and conquer.

If you have an unyielding belief in your ability and in your dreams, and a strong determination to make it a reality, you will be a multi-millionaire very soon. You will then be an idol for many others in the pursuit of success.

And, lastly, if this book has inspired or helped you in any way in your journey to become a multi-millionaire, please write to me at the following address:

SUBHASH LAKHOTIA
Lakhotia Niwas
S-228, Greater Kailash, Phase-II
New Delhi - 110048
Mobile No. 9810001665